ADVANCE

NAIL THE INTERVIEW, LAND THE JOB

Michelle's comprehensive guide hits every phase of the interview process from preparation to follow up. She engages the reader with practical advice, useful tales of job seekers, and tips on successfully navigating the process. The highly digestible book will prove useful not only for our MBA graduates, but also alumni who may be reentering the workplace or in transition.

Regina Resnick, Associate Dean and Managing Director, Career Management Center, Columbia Business School

In today's highly competitive global labor market, job seekers, more than ever, need to master the art of interviewing for a job. In *Nail the Interview, Land the Job*, Michelle Tillis Lederman provides a wealth of information to help individuals successfully navigate the often-stressful task of interviewing for a job. The insightful tips and resources will help new graduates land their first job, as well as seasoned workers who are back in the market.

Bill Castellano, Ph.D., Associate Dean, Rutgers University School of Management and Labor Relations

The recession has resulted in many highly qualified unemployed people who can make finding that next job and selling yourself in the interview difficult. Michelle's book, *Nail the Interview, Land the Job,* will enable you to navigate the challenging questions with ease. Her insights move you from mind-set to interview day to follow up to help you cultivate the results you want in tough times.

Rajesh Setty, Serial Entrepreneur, Author of 15 books including *Gratitude: Changing the World One Thank You at a Time*

Nail the Interview, Land the Job not only gives you brass tacks but also a perspective of both sides of the interview process. As someone who recently went through the process, I know firsthand that looking for and landing a job is utterly frustrating, if not depressing. Michelle helps keep both your attitude and your to-do's on track.

Alyssa Dver, Author of *Kickass Confident: Own Your Brain. Up Your Game* **and CEO, American Confidence Institute**

Michelle has created the definitive guide to nailing your job interviews, whether you're interviewing for an internal or an external position. Michelle's advice is top notch and comprehensive, including nuanced advice to those entering the market or reentering after an extended or unintended leave. I really wish I had her tips on how to field the many challenging, unexpected, and, at times, even inappropriate questions I've fielded over my many years of being an interviewee. Her tips are gold!

John Corcoran, Chief Revolutionary, SmartBusinessRevolution.com

Michelle is the interviewer and candidate's dream alike, illustrating in practical detail not only how to make it through the selection process but also how to make sure your employer sees you as a potential all-star instead of a liability. I'll be sharing this book with everyone in my life who's in transition, whether they're looking for their first job or moving up to the c-suite.

Jordan Harbinger, Host of The Art of Charm

Looking for a complete guide to effective interviewing? Look no further. Michelle Lederman's *Nail the Interview, Land the Job* offers interview tips, tricks, and strategies to effectively land your next position. After years prepping hundreds of candidates seeking an internal promotion or a brand-new role, I know that this is just the type of must-have manual that will help anyone impress a hiring manager and win their dream role.

Denise Brosseau, CEO, Thought Leadership Lab and Author of *Ready to Be a Thought Leader?*

The overwhelming noise in the marketplace too often invades the job-interview process. In *Nail the Interview, Land the Job*, Michelle cuts through the chaos by providing clear steps and structures to manage the end-to-end interview process. She simplifies even those challenging circumstances that many returning parents, young graduates, and laid-off candidates face. A must-have guide for the job seeker at any stage of his or her career.

Linda Popky, Author of *Marketing Above the Noise: Achieve Strategic Advantage with Marketing that Matters*

Interviews position us for advancement. Michelle Lederman is one of those unique, sensitive professionals who truly understands the strategies that move interviews from unproductive meetings to conversations that grab the other person to want to know more about us. Her warm, smart, engaging instructions and examples provide the know-how like no one I have ever spoken with. These tips extend beyond the interview to on the job! There are many books on the topic out there. But none with the clarity and punch of *Nail the Interview, Land the Job*. Read this book and get ready for your first day on the job!

Karen Kahn, Psychologist, Strategic Coach for Lawyers, and Author of *Daunting to DOable: You CAN Make It Rain*

I'm constantly asked by my university students how to prepare for an interview so they can get a great job, and Michelle's book is a perfect resource for them. Her years of experience on both sides of the interview desk and overall business savvy give her a unique perspective on how to fully prepare for any type of interview from standard to virtual to the unconventional. She reveals all the interviewer secrets, tricks, and tools needed to be successful in making your next career move.

Whitney Keyes, Professor and Author of *Propel: Five Ways to Amp Up Your Marketing and Accelerate Business*

If you are looking for a new job or are fresh out of school, you NEED this book. You will do just what the title says—nail the Interview! Michelle's writing style really grabs you. Her conversational approach—full of great storytelling, examples, and case studies—makes *Nail the Interview, Land the Job* a quick, easy read for everyone. She shares plenty of specific tips for young graduates to reentrants to out-of-work executives. It is a must-read for anyone in the market for a job or a job change.

Jan Fox, Television Journalist and Four-time Emmy Winner

Interviewing for a new position can be filled with moments of nervousness and self-doubt. Michelle has done an outstanding job in offering practical advice and a road map to approaching these opportunities with the greatest possible confidence. Her conversational style and willingness to share personal experiences offers the reader a genuine sense of humility as the pages are turned. Whether you are a recent grad, returning to the workforce, or recently unemployed, *Nail the Interview, Land the Job* is the confidence builder that will allow you to bring your A game to the table.

Bill McLean, Partner, Consulting (Leadership Development), PwC Canada

NAIL THE
INTERVIEW
LAND THE JOB

NAIL THE INTERVIEW
LAND THE JOB

A STEP-BY-STEP GUIDE
FOR WHAT TO DO
BEFORE, DURING, AND
AFTER THE INTERVIEW

MICHELLE TILLIS LEDERMAN

SHORTi
PRESS

Nail the Interview, Land the Job
A Step-by-Step Guide for What to Do Before, During, and After the Interview
By Michelle Tillis Lederman
Shorti Press

Published by Shorti Press, South Orange, New Jersey
Printed in the United States of America.

Editor: Meeghan Truelove
Cover Design: Estela Jia Ceyril Redulla
Interior Design and Layout: Yvonne Parks at www.PearCreative.ca

Library of Congress Control Number: 2015909689

ISBN: 978-0-9965078-0-6

This book is dedicated to my family, always,
and to all those who have the courage to design their ideal.

TABLE OF CONTENTS

ACKNOWLEDGMENTS

There are so many people who have helped make this book complete. My first, last, and biggest thanks must always go to my family. Michael, thank you for dealing with my insane and unconventional approach to work and life—you make it so much more crazy and fun. James and Noah, thank you for making me feel good and not guilty about being a working mother. The fact that you two are proud of me is my fuel.

My family has always supported me in everything I do, and I thank them all: my mother, my father, my sister, my nieces and nephews, and my amazing in-laws—I love being a part of this family and all the ways it extends.

Rebecca Rodskog and Abby Katoni (my people), I trust and value your perspectives more than you know. Thank you for being the best sounding boards.

Meeghan Truelove, my editor and my friend, you know my voice and help ensure my message is clear. You make my work so much better— thank you. Thanks also for introducing me to Amanda Woytus, a great and much-needed copy editor and proofreader.

Thank you to Janica Smith, whom I call my general contractor of book production and the queen of the Shorti Press team. Thank you to my "authoresses," who have shared much-needed insight and encouragement.

The phrase "it takes a village" applies to my life in so many ways. I thank all those who have been a part and will be a part of my village throughout my life.

INTRODUCTION

Congratulations! You've landed the interview. That means a company or potential employer has already identified something in you that they like, and they want to meet you. You applied online, used a headhunter, showed up in person to fill out an application, went through career services, or used your network to secure an in. However you did it, you had the confidence to throw your hat in the ring. Now it's time to focus on the task at hand—the interview—to give you the best chance of getting the job. I always say, "Get the job first, then decide if you want it." Let taking the job be your decision. But in order to get the job, you must ace the interview. And that is exactly what I am here to help you do.

Changing careers, seeking work after a layoff, entering the workforce for the first time, or returning to work after taking time off to be a parent can all be daunting prospects. Each of these groups faces a unique set of challenges, expectations, and demands. As you go through the job-interview process, you may need to acclimate to certain conventions, environments, and codes of behavior that are new or have been idle for you, and to challenge yourself in unexpected ways. Preparation, clarity, and confidence will go a long way in the interview process and will ultimately lead to exactly what you want to achieve: getting a job!

In this book I will address the questions, fears, and mental roadblocks that you may face, and how you can overcome these challenges to excel at the interview process. I'll also shed light on the specific strengths and competitive advantages that you may bring to your next position without even knowing it, and how you can make sure to communicate these qualities to a recruiter or potential employer. It's time to highlight your skills and accomplishments and land your next job!

OVERCOMING LIMITING BELIEFS

Right away, I want to bring up one of the least recognized and most difficult hurdles you may face when going through the interview process: identifying and removing **limiting beliefs**. Do you ever hear yourself thinking things such as the following? "They will never hire someone without experience." "I can't start over at my age." "I've been out of the workforce too long to be a desirable candidate." These are all examples of a limiting belief—in other words, something that you believe to be a fact but is actually nothing more than an assumption.

Everyone has limiting beliefs about one thing or another. New grads may think that they'll have a hard time getting a foot in the door because they don't have any experience or relationships to leverage. Parents returning to the workforce might worry that their decision to take time off will be a strike against them. People who were recently laid off may be struggling with feelings of inadequacy. If you're changing careers, you may assume that you won't be considered for work in a field that is new to you. Although it's normal to feel uncertainty, limiting beliefs confine you and your choices. The good news is that they can be overcome.

The first step to doing this is to recognize when a limiting belief pops into your head. If you want to test a thought for its negativity, ask yourself if you can come up with an example that proves it wrong. Can you think of someone you know who was able to land a job quickly after being laid off, or someone who reentered the workforce after having taken a long time off to be with his or her kids? And wasn't there a time when you yourself did something you had thought you'd never be able to do? It's important to be realistic about what you bring to the table, but it's just as important not to limit yourself based on what you *think* you can't do.

If you're having trouble coming up with a real-life example to test a limiting belief, try asking yourself, "What would it be like if this limiting belief were not true?" Envision this possibility and you will often see that the opposite of a limiting belief is not that big of a stretch. It's not the difference between black and white, truth and fiction, with everything in between gray. It's the difference between one version of a belief and another version of a belief, and all the colors and possibilities in between. We believe our own stories—and if we change a story, we change that belief and liberate ourselves from its limitations.

Another important tip is something that I highlighted in my first book, *The 11 Laws of Likability*: Be your own best friend. In other words, when you're having negative thoughts, tell yourself what you would want a great friend to tell you. Change the self-limiting thoughts, and you'll change the message. Instead of "I can't do that," make the thought, "Once I am on the job I'll learn quickly, and I will be great," or better yet, "I will excel in that role. I just need the chance to show them."

We'll continue looking at limiting beliefs—and how to conquer them—throughout this book. For now, just remember that you *can* nail the interview and you *can* land a great job. The more fully you embrace what's possible, the less limited you will be by any preexisting negative beliefs.

SOME COMMON JOB-TRANSITION CHALLENGES

Throughout the course of this book, we'll examine the core job-transition challenges you may face—especially as they relate to interviewing—and how you can best handle them. Most of these challenges apply to all sorts of job-seekers, but we'll take an even closer look at the specific challenges for these particular groups: new graduates, parents returning from having taken time off, and people who have recently been fired or laid off. For now, let's take a quick look at some of the most common challenges that any of us might face, regardless of where we're coming from.

- **Translating Skills.** One of the biggest job-search challenges can be explaining how your skill sets from previous experiences translate to the type of employment you're currently seeking. Whether you're moving from one industry to another or from volunteer work to a paid position, you might worry that you haven't yet established enough of a track record to pull off that transition. The trick is to identify the skills that are relevant from any previous experience you've had and communicate those in your interview.

A good place to start is to think about what you did on a daily basis in your previous environment. For instance, parents returning to the workforce are coming from full-time childcare situations—those require quick thinking, resourceful problem solving, and excellent communication skills. Parents have to be adaptable, energetic, and creative; they have to be masters at managing logistics and coordinating schedules; they have to pay attention to detail and communicate critical information clearly. As the parent of elementary school–age kids, I know that I face this all the time. I have to explain difficult concepts, find ways to make practicing an instrument and doing homework more fun, and cajole my kids into trying new foods without them catching on too much. I know many moms who don't realize how hard they work on a daily basis planning events, helping with school activities, or marketing fund-raisers. Because they are not paid, often they—and society—devalue the skills that are required.

As a new grad, your lack of professional experience might actually work in your favor. For an interviewer, the passion and confidence that you project as an interviewee can often be much more powerful than what's on your résumé. As a recent grad, not only do you probably project enthusiasm and an eagerness to learn and prove yourself, but you have also just left an environment where you were studying the most recent developments in your field. You might be more aware of the latest advances and technologies than many of the people at the place where you are applying to work. And you've got a fresh perspective and energy that you can bring to any problem solving.

The first step in preparing for an interview is to recognize these skills that you already possess, and the second step is to value them and understand how to translate them. You want to be able to communicate how these skills translate to the job for which you're applying at every step of the process, from résumé and cover letter right through to the actual interview.

- **Overcoming Negative Biases.** You may be concerned that certain facts about your background or identity will be strikes against you: your age, your gender, your ethnicity, gaps in your work history, or your lack of previous experience. If you've been laid off, you may feel pink slip stigma about it, and you may feel that you must have done something wrong to be the one they got rid of—even though you know the boss cut you because your earning level exceeded that of everyone else. Remember that there are many reasons for layoffs. During the recession, one of my neighbors was laid off not because of his performance, but because the law firm he worked for decided to refocus on core areas that didn't include his area of expertise. Understand your story so that you can project the right message.

If you're a new grad, you might worry that your interviewer will assume you don't understand professional etiquette. You might also be nervous that because you lack experience, your interviewer will doubt that you know what it means to have a strong work ethic.

Biases do exist—we all have them—but here's the problem with walking into an interview assuming that the interviewer already has you figured out in the most negative possible ways: You risk presenting yourself as someone with a chip on his or her shoulder. In fact, you may very well be bringing biases into a room where before there were none! Which means that you need to overcome your own biases inwardly, so that you don't project them outwardly.

Instead of immediately thinking the worst of your interviewer, assume that he or she has no preconceived judgments about you. Assume that they are thinking what you want them to think: Project the right messages. If you keep an open mind, the interviewer is extremely likely to do the same.

If you do feel as though you're coming up against biases at an interview, stay focused on demonstrating who you are as a specific person, and what you will uniquely bring to the position.

- **Projecting confidence and positioning yourself.** One of the most challenging aspects of the job-search and interviewing process is managing self-doubt. We've all got it, especially if we're new to the workforce, counting unemployment in months, changing careers, or reentering the workforce after speaking toddler talk for years. How do you present yourself to ensure that your interviewer can see you fitting into the company?

At the end of the day, if you don't think you can do it, nobody else will think you can, either. You'll need to convince others with your voice, with your body language, and with your story. So you'll need to convince yourself first. The story needs to be authentic: If you believe it, others will believe it, too.

The most important thing for you to remember—and moms out there, this one goes especially to you—is that no apologies are necessary. You have made good choices. Whether you accepted the buyout package, didn't pursue a particular promotion, traveled after school instead of finding a steady job, shifted into the slow lane for a while, or left the workforce entirely, you made the right choice for you. As a person who is ready to work now and knows what that means—whether from previous employment experience or through hard work at school—you are coming from a position of strength.

SPECIAL CONSIDERATIONS AND CHALLENGES

It's challenging to look for work, no matter what your situation is. But if you're a new grad, have been laid off recently, or are a parent returning to the workforce after a substantial time off, there may be some additional factors to consider. Thinking about these things before going into the interview can positively impact how you handle them once the interview is underway.

Fit and flexibility. This is a challenge particularly apt for parents returning to work. How will a new job fit in with raising a family? Moms and dads often need a work culture with some flexibility. Will you sound like a potential problem employee if during the interview you ask questions about on-site childcare or company policies regarding telecommuting and flexible hours? How can you show that you are right for the job if you are up against a younger worker with fewer responsibilities? We will dive into these questions—and how to nail your answers to them—in Chapters 5 through 9. Some workplaces won't be good matches, and you need to find that out, but not during the first interview. Our credo throughout this book is, Get the job first!

Culture shock. New grads and career switchers may not be accustomed to the culture of an unfamiliar workplace. Corporate offices have etiquette and protocols. One thing these kinds of employers are looking for is whether or not they can put you in front of a client. Polish and professionalism in your dress, mannerisms, and word choice will go a long way toward communicating that you are indeed fit for the job. If you're green, a company will of course give you *some* slack. But do your research so that you can at least show that you're already making an effort. Try to figure out if the company has a casual or formal dress code. I know one new grad who didn't wear a tie to an interview at a law firm—big mistake! Another young grad I know went to an interview at a public relations firm and brought samples of his design work in a portfolio that featured a competitor's logo, a gift from a summer internship. He didn't get the job, either.

Networking. If you've been out of the workforce for a while, you may think that you have no ability to network. The reality is that we all actively network all the time, whether we know it or not. And your network is actually larger than you think, because each contact we have has a whole set of his or her own contacts. For new grads, your entire school and alumni association are part of your active network, though really school connections like these are pertinent for anyone looking for a job. Search on LinkedIn and reach out to alumni at a firm or in a field you are interested in. They may have valuable insights and connections that they are willing to share. Most universities have groups on LinkedIn and Facebook. Consider posting questions there and see who responds.

If you're a mom or dad, your parent network is stronger than you know. I found one of my best clients through my kids' kindergarten. Just because you no longer work at a company doesn't mean you don't have a network. Even if you were laid off or fired, you likely still have good relationships with many people at your former place of employment. Think broadly. Networking doesn't have to feel like you're doing something—it's really just about building relationships. It's not, "Can you help me get a job?" It's, "Can we get a cup of coffee?"

Awkwardly qualified. If you're unemployed, you're right to cast your net wide and perhaps even think about switching careers. You might be considering jobs for which you are overqualified in some ways and underqualified in others. In a certain sense, you're asking the company to take a leap of faith in hiring you. They might fear that you're not serious, that you're just trying something out, that you don't really want to take a pay cut. You'll have to work hard in the interview to prove that you'll stick around and give it your all, but this is doable. When you are facing an unconventional fit, it is critical to keep in mind that confidence is as important as competence.

The truth is that there are no hard and fast rules for getting an interview right, but there are extremely helpful guidelines for it, and there are concrete things you can do at every step along the way to improve your odds of securing a job. And I'm going to show you how.

THREE TRUE TALES: A NEW GRAD, A RETURNING MOM, AND A LAID-OFF EMPLOYEE

There are times when landing a job can be particularly challenging, and we'll address those situations—and how to troubleshoot them— throughout this book. But everywhere you look, there are real-life stories of people who have found fulfilling work despite the odds. Some of them, I promise you, are even in your own network of family, friends, and colleagues. Before we dive into the book in earnest, I thought I'd share three stories from my own life that demonstrate how it's always possible to find work that's the right fit for you.

The New Grad

Recent grads are often new to interviewing and lack practice, but perseverance and passion can be enough to propel them in the right professional direction. I have a childhood friend named Jeff whose career track I'm in awe of. He was always crazy about music, but he was never a great student. When he graduated from college, he knew his dream of working for a record label was out of reach. He wasn't qualified—yet. But he didn't let these limitations stop him. Instead he let his passion fuel his path, and it ultimately catapulted him to the top of the music industry. Here's how he tells his story:

"In college, I needed a job. Most of my friends worked in bars, but this didn't make sense to me. 'Where's the music industry?' I asked myself. At a record store! So that's where I worked. I learned the business from the ground up. I did sales reporting, inventory, music buying, and, most importantly, I talked up every label and distribution rep who came into the store.

"One day, I struck up a relationship with a person on the phone, who was in radio ad sales, interviewed with that company, and landed a job before I'd even graduated. I found there one of the most influential mentors of my career. While this was going on, I was also one of Atlantic Records' college reps, distributing posters and stickers and flyers all over town.

"Post-graduation, I wanted to be even deeper inside the music industry, so I made a bold move, left the marketing company while still maintaining a strong relationship with them, and went back to the record store. Very humbling, but I knew it's where I'd have access to label reps. I was making calls, sending résumés, and interviewing, and I landed my first label gig at I.R.S. Records as operations manager. It was a nonmusic role, but I was 24 years old and full of energy and enthusiasm, and I learned it all— sales calls, radio station visits, press releases, media alerts, sales reporting. I hung out with and did promo for so many bands it was unreal.

"From there, I moved on to the vanguard of the music industry's dot-com. This in turn led to 10 years as a senior director for one of the biggest music labels in the world. I've worked with some of the most amazing artists on the planet, from Norah Jones and Wynton Marsalis to Willie Nelson and the Beastie Boys. It's been a dream come true."

The Returning Parent

If you're a parent who is returning to the workforce after spending time being a stay-at-home mom or dad, it can be intimidating to jump back into those waters. You may think that your time away has killed any chances you could have had in your field, or you may feel as if you haven't been gaining experience while away from employment.

My friend Felice, who lives in my community, was able to successfully reenter the working world after almost seven years away because she leveraged her contacts and viewed her stay-at-home-mom time as actual valuable experience. I always called her the hardest-working unpaid person I knew, but it was exactly that mentality that helped her transition so fluidly back into the workforce. When she was ready to look for work, she had clarity about the kind of role she was seeking, and she overcame the assumptions that she wouldn't find anything because she'd been out of the game. Even though she didn't have any idea how to go about finding a job after so long away, she started sharing her aspirations with family and friends, most of whom were still in the workforce. Before long, her extensive personal network kicked in and an opportunity floated to the surface. According to Felice:

"I'd been running special events for a Wall Street firm when I got laid off. I was pregnant with my second child, and so it just seemed to make sense to do the stay-at-home-mom thing for a while. I don't think I ever spent a full day 'staying at home.' I was constantly on the go: volunteering, serving as the president of my kids' preschool, helping friends and other families in our community by organizing playdates and picking kids up from school, et cetera. When my husband got laid off after more than two decades at the same bank, we knew it was time for me to go back to work. One day a friend of mine called to say that she'd attended an event at a new conference center, and she nudged me to reach out to them and apply for a job. Long story short, I'm now the general manager of that conference center. I absolutely love it. And I never would have found the position if I hadn't put it out there that I was looking for a particular job."

The Laid-Off Employee

There's no doubt that losing your job can be a devastating experience, but one of the most powerful things you can do in this situation is look not at what you've lost, but what you've gained. What are the opportunities that have suddenly opened up to you? What are the things that you've always wanted to do? Finding employment after being laid off requires a combo of the skills and attitudes highlighted in the New Grads and Returning Parents sections above: Connect with your passion, get clear, and talk about it with everyone you know.

For the first part of my life, I was a CPA. That was miserable, so I went to business school and, upon graduation, landed a job at a top consulting firm. The position had prestige, but the reality of the work was not what I thought it would be, and I dreaded going to the office. One day we had a company-wide "impact" day, for which I was responsible for three public schools in Harlem. It was one of the best days of my life, and it was a revelation for me. I told one of the partners that I wanted to give up my client work and do corporate social responsibility work for the company instead. After she looked into it, she later told me there was no such position. Little did I know, the company had been going through layoff rounds—and I basically raised my hand and said that I didn't like the work. Soon after, I was laid off. I was stunned and upset—for about a day. As it turned out, that was actually when my professional life began.

I got let go on a Monday. Tuesday I cleaned out my desk and called a friend who worked in banking. He told me to come work for him, even though he was in a completely different field. Wednesday I went in and interviewed with him. Thursday I interviewed with his boss, the bank's treasurer. That following Monday I started as a contractor, reporting directly to the treasurer. It wasn't my dream job, but it was fine, and I was learning tons. Eventually the treasurer got promoted to a position in Tokyo. He asked me to come with him and help him transition. I hired a coach to assist and on that trip figured out what I was meant to do. I wanted to teach, coach, improve workplace communications, design trainings—have an impact. For three years, I developed those skills on the side while I still held down my finance job, and then I went out on my own and never looked back.

I traveled lots of different paths before I finally connected with my professional passion. Along the way, I could have had a pity party, but instead I always asked myself, "What's the good side of all this?" I reached out to my network, and I kept going until I found what, for me, was meaningful work. Getting laid off was the best thing that could have ever happened to me. I was ready to take risks because I was already in a place of risk. It was that turning point that gave me the chance to eventually pivot toward what I really wanted to do. It was a gift.

THE INTERVIEW PROCESS

Regardless of the industry or position you are pursuing, there are typically five phases to an interview. The stages may happen in a different order from interview to interview, but a well-structured interview will include these five essential components:

- **Rapport Building.** This happens throughout an interview, but you have the most potential to create a positive rapport with the interviewer during the first few minutes. Building rapport helps you get a sense of the interviewer's personality, and it breaks the ice, which will help you manage your nerves and set the tone for the interview. Smile and greet the person with a handshake. Likability is key!

- **Introductory Question.** The interviewer may move seamlessly from chitchat into the first question. The opening query is often a broad overview request and is intended to be easy. This can allow you to settle into the interview and increase your comfort level.

- **Core.** The core is the substantive segment of the interview, when the interviewer gathers the most relevant information about you. During this phase, the interviewer is trying to determine three things:

  1. Do you have the skills to do the job?

  2. Do you have the interest/passion/desire to do the job?

  3. Will you fit with the people and culture of the company?

- **Candidate Q&A.** At some point during the interview, the prospective employer will turn it over to you to ask questions. This is your opportunity to learn more about the company, its employees, and the specific job you're interviewing for.

- **Closing.** The last part of the interview is when you ensure that you've communicated everything you want the interviewer to know about you. Before you leave, you also want to understand the next steps in the process and the best timing and methods for following up.

In the following nine chapters, you will learn all the skills you need to navigate the interview process with intelligence, grace, and authenticity. I'll give you specific advice for every step of the process, from pre-interview preparations to asking and answering interview questions to effectively following up. Throughout the book we'll pay special attention to the needs of the various categories of candidates mentioned above, but much of the material will resonate for all job seekers, regardless of experience level or current employment status. Although much of the content focuses on office positions, these tips can be applied for any job interview, whether your desired job is in the corporate world or not.

Now, let's get started.

THE PRE-INTERVIEW PREP

CHAPTER 1:
STOP PLAYING MIND GAMES!
GET INTO THE INTERVIEW MIND-SET

Once you've secured an interview, you're excited, you're elated! And then your mind starts playing games, tampering with the confidence you very much need. To prepare for an interview in the best possible way, it is critical to identify the mind games you are playing and then tell your mind, "Game over." Which mind games below apply to you?

THE GAMES WE PLAY

Taboo: You are stricken by the fear that you will say or do the wrong thing, and with one false move you will suddenly lose everything that is at stake. This is a common mind game played by fired and laid-off candidates. Not only are you struggling to spin the occurrence in a positive light, but you may also be managing strong emotions with how you were treated during the job-termination process. You second-guess your responses and as a result, project a lack of confidence. Doubt and hesitation reign.

Charades: You begin changing how you'll act based on what you think the interviewer is looking for, altering your behavior to try to be the candidate you think he or she wants. This is a common mind game, especially for the newly graduated. You are playing a role. You might imagine what the company's dream candidate is and then try shoehorning yourself into that persona. The problem is that this can read as arrogance, exactly the opposite of what an entry-level person should be projecting, and it compromises your authenticity. New grads need to strike a balance between conveying a strong sense of self and an understanding that they still have a lot to learn. Drop the facade you are using to hide your lack of experience. Instead, use your newness to your advantage. Attitude is paramount to aptitude—the correct new hire can learn the skills he or she needs to know, but a bad attitude is much harder to change.

Sorry: You assume that you are not worthy of the employment opportunity, that you don't have the correct qualifications, and in your head you are already apologizing for your occasional absence from the workforce—a typical game played by returning parents and the unemployed. You feel as if you have to defend your decisions and make excuses for having been out of the workforce for so long. As a result, you tend to assume that the interviewer is judging you for your choices and circumstances. You may assume that the interviewer has already turned against you. The problem with this is that you'll quickly position yourself as an adversary rather than an ally.

All these mind games can be crippling and destructive. If you are riddled with fear, feel apologetic about who you are, or think that you need to be someone else, you are endangering your chance of finding a true, fulfilling job match.

So what mind game *should* you be playing as you prepare for the interview?

Truth or Dare: As I detailed in my book *The 11 Laws of Likability* (*www. the11lawsoflikability.com*), authenticity is the key to making meaningful connections. It is also, without a doubt, the most crucial part of successful interviewing. In order to ace that interview, you need to be who you really are. Be honest in your answers. Without honest responses, it will be impossible for you and the interviewer to determine if you are a good match for the job.

I had a student when I was teaching at New York University who asked if I would conduct a mock interview with him. I said sure. So I sat with him and we chitchatted, and he was perfectly warm and friendly, but as soon as I started asking real interview-type questions, he stiffened up, lost his smile, and changed his tone. It was so obvious that he was playing a game of charades. I tried to trick him into thinking I wasn't interviewing him, but as soon as he figured out this tactic, the mask came back. In order to go through an interview successfully and truly stand out, it is critical that you trust yourself and dare to be the real you.

When you heed this advice to "be yourself," you might not get the job—and that's for the best. During business school, I landed an interview at an elite consulting firm. Needless to say, I was thrilled. I really wanted the job. During my initial interview, a senior executive challenged me with a case study. I asked him a question, and he enthusiastically exclaimed, "You're the only person who has asked me that all day!" He was clearly delighted, and I knew I'd secured a second interview. After the second interview I secured a third one, and so on. Each time I felt more convinced than ever that the job was mine. I was being completely authentic in those interviews—animated and energetic and fully myself.

After my seventh round of interviews they sat me down, praised my intelligence and critical-thinking skills, and told me that I didn't get the job. I was shocked. "Why?" I asked. They said that my style was too casual. I was devastated—for about an hour. And then I started thinking about it. Thank *goodness* I didn't get the job. If they had offered it to me, I absolutely would have accepted it, and I would not have fit in with the company culture. It would have stifled and frustrated me and wasted who knows how many years of my professional life. The moral of this story for me has always been this: You have to be you. It is the only way you are going to avoid jobs for which you're ill suited and instead find the positions that will let you flourish and grow.

KNOWLEDGE, CLARITY, CONFIDENCE

So how do you combat the silly games your mind can play? By being fully prepared for an interview. Getting ready for an interview is a chain reaction, which I think of as Knowledge, Clarity, Confidence. As you gain understanding about a job, you become clearer about the professional opportunity it presents and your possible role in it, and your strengths naturally come to the fore.

Knowledge

Knowledge is power. Know yourself, your target company, and your industry. Gather the most useful information, engage your curiosity, go deep. Use your network to find friends and contacts who may be familiar with the industry or company you are pursuing. Tap into programs in your community and place of worship, or chambers of commerce that provide networking opportunities, talks, and other events related to your field. Consider joining or attending sessions organized by professional or industry groups that may be relevant to you and your targeted employer.

Research what the media and financial analysts are saying about the company and industry. Use Google to get a baseline of information, and then get firsthand accounts: Network, visit job fairs to talk directly with people in your desired field. Job fairs are an excellent resource, designed to inform you about the day-to-day realities of various industries. Check out the bonus section at the end of this book for more on career fairs.

If you've set your sights on a particular company, see if you can find out how it has fared over the past several quarters. What alliances has the company formed? What nonprofits does it support? What associations are the employees members of? Delving into these topics will give you a better sense of the company's culture, what factors make it successful, and the obstacles it may face. It will also help you develop your strategy for the interview and formulate the questions you want to be sure you ask.

You can learn the answers to many of your questions by simply going to the company's website. Companies also often have Facebook, Twitter, and LinkedIn pages. You can start a conversation or post a comment, and your name may be known before you walk in the door. Use your high school and college's alumni networks to dig deeper, and call your college's career services department to find out what they might know. Visit the library to search LexisNexis for news articles or business filings, and Dow Jones for more information on a company and to see whom their competitors are. Most public libraries and all college libraries have free access to these databases, and the librarians can help you navigate them.

Clarity

As you prepare for an interview, you need to focus on figuring out if the job you're applying for is a good fit for you, and if the company you're interviewing with is a desirable employer. You also must get clear about what you can bring to the job, and the image you want to project during the interview.

The Role: A great place to start understanding the role for which you're interviewing is to get as familiar as possible with the official job description. Make a list of what the company states it is looking for in the job description, and don't get discouraged if you can't tick all the boxes on the list. The point here is to emphasize the ways in which you're a good match for the position, not dwell on the ways you might not be. Make notes about your skills and how they are relevant for the position. Think broadly and include *attributes* (qualities or characteristics, such as "initiative" or "confidence"), *behaviors* (actions or reactions, such as "challenges the status quo" or "mentors others"), and *competencies* (the knowledge, skills, or abilities required, such as "communication," "industry familiarity," or "technical proficiency").

If you have access to someone who works or has worked for the company, ask him or her about the prevailing corporate culture and anything you may need to know that wasn't listed in the job description.

Your Preferences: Getting clear about what you are looking for in a job is critical for two reasons. First, if you know precisely why a job is a good fit for you, you will be better prepared to communicate this to the interviewer. Second, if you understand that a position will be a good fit for you, you'll feel confident about landing in a situation that lets you thrive. If you're happy, you'll be the most productive and successful. Understand the type of work you want to do, the industry you want to be a part of, and your optimal work-life balance. The work-life balance issue has always been on the list for parents returning to the workforce, but it's been noted as of serious importance for millennials, too. I personally knew I didn't want to work crazy hours and specifically chose a field I felt was more reasonable than a hard-core finance job.

It is critical that you identify your employment preferences as thoroughly as possible. In workplace culture, you need to have a clear idea of what you might specifically want to do, based on what you uniquely bring to the table. Don't confuse being flexible with not having a clear message. You need to show not just that you can do the job but also that you truly want to.

Your Skills: Getting clear about the skills and strengths you bring to an organization can be a difficult step in the process. You must remember that you have many assets that will draw employers to you. The crux is to determine which specific strengths are the most applicable for a particular job, and then project those strengths in a genuine way during the interview.

To help you identify your most valuable and relevant skills and characteristics, complete the following activity.

Activity: Identify Your Three Words

What specific traits, qualities, or skills would make you effective in a potential role? Compile a list of all the words that could apply. Ask people who know you well to add words to the list. Review the attributes that you've come up with against those that others have used to describe you. Where is the overlap? Rank these qualities in order of strength.

Go back to the work you did to determine what would make someone successful in this role based on the official job description and your research on the company. Make a list of those attributes, ordering them by how relevant and desirable they are to the employer. Compare this list to the list you compiled of your particular strengths, and select the first three traits that appear on both lists. Be sure that they highlight different positive aspects of your personality and compatibility for the role—if it seems like there is too much overlap, keep comparing the lists until you've identified three distinct attributes. For example, don't choose three synonyms such as hardworking, diligent, and efficient even if they appear on both lists as they are basically saying the same thing about you. You also want to look for words on both lists that describe how you manage and interact with others, and touch on different aspects of how you approach your work.

These words that you've chosen are your "three words," and they are critical to conveying your strengths as a candidate. These are the words that you feel most connected to, that would represent you at your best in this new position, and they are the three qualities that you are going to make absolutely sure you project to the interviewer. We'll refer to your "three words"—and how to use them to the greatest effect—throughout this book.

Confidence

All the knowledge and clarity you've been building will help you establish a more complete picture of what the job you're after demands and—most importantly—how your skills match the open position. In order to enter an interview with confidence, you must believe that you possess the necessary skills and have the ability to be successful in the position. It is rare that prior skill sets will be an exact match when the position in question is a brand-new endeavor, but it is entirely possible—and in fact crucial—to figure out *how* your skill sets apply to the new situation.

The process of translating your skills is a matter of recognizing the extraordinary experience you've acquired, even if that experience is raising kids, succeeding in college, or your tenure at a previous job. Discipline, loyalty, critical thinking, problem solving, decision making, adaptability, creativity, the ability to perform under pressure, managing time and stress, relationship building, and communication skills are just a few of the assets that have immediate, ready value. If the person interviewing you doesn't immediately see how your experiences, passion, and personality are a fit for the position, it is your responsibility to make sure they know it by the end of the interview. The main challenge will be perception—yours and theirs. Believe in your capabilities and qualifications, and you will communicate this to others.

GENDER GAP

As a woman, I was curious about how differences in confidence levels play out in research between men and women. Again and again, I found research concluding that women are less self-assured than men—and that to succeed in the professional world, confidence matters as much as competence. Women, awareness of this disparity is the first step toward fully embracing your confidence. Here are some of the things I uncovered:

- A 2011 study by the United Kingdom's Institute of Leadership and Management queried professional managers about their confidence levels. Half of the women polled said they experienced self-doubt regarding their performance and career; less than a third of the men polled reported these same self-doubts.

- While studying business school students, Linda Babcock, an economics professor at Carnegie Mellon University and the author of *Women Don't Ask*, discovered that men ask for salary increases four times more often than women do, and that when women do ask for a raise, they ask for 30 percent less money than the men do.

- Studies by Cornell and Washington State universities have revealed that while men tend to overestimate their abilities and performances, women underestimate themselves.

- While writing their book *Womenomics*, Claire Shipman and Katty Kay noted that when discussing why they felt they weren't moving forward in their careers, women tended toward some level of self-deprecation. Shipman herself mentioned "luck" as a factor in her own career successes, despite an impressive résumé.

So what does this mean for us women? It means awareness is the first thing, but change is the next. Here are a few tips to close this gap:

1. **Say Yes.** When asked if you want to do something, don't talk yourself out of it or question your ability. Say yes, then figure out how to get it done. You always do.

2. **Use the 80/20 Rule.** Don't worry if you aren't 100 percent sure, have 100 percent of the qualifications, or if the task you've just completed is 100 percent perfect. Use the 80/20 rule. If you are 80 percent there, go for it. Done is better than perfect.

3. **Act.** Don't overthink it. Get out of your head and get into action.

4. **Ask.** If you don't ask, the answer is no. If you ask, you immediately increase your odds.

5. **Negotiate.** Don't ever take the first offer. Follow tip number 4 and ask for something. And while you are at it, ask for more than you actually want to leave yourself some negotiating room.

The final part of the knowledge, clarity, confidence continuum comes when you take the clarity you've achieved and identify exactly what it is that you want the interviewer to know about you, without any doubts. Don't force it—remember, you're not playing charades or Sorry. You don't want to pretend to be someone other than who you are, and you don't want to apologize for what you have or haven't done. Believe in what you are communicating and be confident about what you bring to the table. If you don't believe in what you're conveying, no one else will, either.

REFRESH YOUR MEMORY

- To fully prepare for an interview, it is critical to identify the mind games you are playing with yourself and then counter them with clear thinking.

- Authenticity is the key to making meaningful connections and a crucial part of successful interviewing. Be honest in your answers, step outside your comfort zone, let go of uniformity, and dare to be the true you.

- Getting ready for an interview is a chain reaction of building knowledge, clarity, and confidence. As you gain understanding about a job, your strengths and qualifications naturally come to the fore.

- Knowledge is power. Gather information about yourself, your target company, your industry. Go deep.

- Get clear about what you can bring to the job, and the image you want to project during the interview.

- Determine the three top qualities you want to convey to the interviewer—these are your "three words." They are the words that you feel most connected to and would represent you at your best in this new position.

- Believe in what you are communicating and be confident about what you bring to the table. If you don't believe in what you're conveying, no one else will, either.

CHAPTER 2:
PRESENTING YOUR BEST SELF
WHAT TO WEAR, WHAT TO BRING, WHAT ELSE TO DO

Now that your mind is in the game and you've put in the advance work to gain knowledge, clarity, and confidence, it's time to focus on planning some specifics: what to wear to the interview, what to bring with you, and what else you need to do to get yourself ready. Preparing in advance will help you minimize distractions and ensure that you maximize the positive impression you make during your interview.

First and foremost, appearances matter. How you present yourself speaks volumes about your attitude and indicates how you will represent and reflect on the company if you're hired. It is critical that you sort out the details of what you're going to wear, from head to toe, well before the day of the interview. You don't want last-minute outfit decisions to distract you from the task at hand: landing the job. We'll drill down on some interview-wardrobe specifics later on in this chapter, but before we do, I want to address another—and increasingly significant—kind of appearance: your online presence.

ADVANCE PREPARATIONS: YOUR ONLINE IMAGE

Everyone knows that first impressions are important. Understanding very clearly exactly what impression you want to make is the first step toward doing so, and the true power of the "Identify Your Three Words" activity. In the next few chapters, we will take in-depth looks at other aspects of making a positive first impression in person and presenting a consistent image.

But before you can create a positive impression in person, you need to score an interview so that you get the opportunity to create a positive in-person impression. A crucial piece of this is managing your online presence so that it doesn't unwittingly tell the wrong story about you before you even get your foot in the door.

According to a 2014 Jobvite Job Seeker Nation Study—an authoritative survey of people who have used social and mobile media to find jobs— 94 percent of recruiters use, or plan to use, social media for recruiting. This number has increased steadily for the past six years. A 2014 Aberdeen Group study found that 73 percent of 18–34-year-olds first heard about their most recent jobs through a social network. A 2014 Career Builder survey revealed that 51 percent of employers rejected job applicants based on what was uncovered about them on social networking sites, up from 43 percent in 2013 and 34 percent in 2012. The offending content posted by candidates included:

- Provocative or inappropriate photos or information

- References to drinking, illegal drugs, or sex
- Bad-mouthing or sharing confidential information about previous employers
- Discriminatory comments about such things as race, gender, or religion
- Evidence of poor communication skills
- Misrepresentation of employment qualifications
- Use of profanity
- Linked to criminal behavior
- Screen name was unprofessional
- Lied about an absence

Conversely, in a survey from U.S. News & World Report, 86 percent of employers indicated that a good online reputation can positively influence a hiring decision. In the 2014 CareerBuilder survey, one-third of employers who research candidates on social networking sites say they've found content that made them more likely to hire a candidate. What's more, nearly a quarter found content that directly led to them hiring the candidate. Here are a few ways to leverage the power of your online image:

- Change your email address to something that sounds professional.
- Delete inappropriate materials from your social media accounts.
- Change your privacy settings to ensure that you know who is seeing what on your social media accounts.
- Create a LinkedIn profile that enhances your résumé.
- Post a professional head-and-shoulders picture of yourself in your social media profiles.
- Follow people on Twitter who are in your field of interest.

- Create a Google Alert for your name so you'll know whenever material about you appears online.

Per CareerBuilder, here are some of the most common reasons employers hired a candidate based on their social networking presence:

- Got a good feel for the job candidate's personality; could see a good fit within the company culture
- Job candidate's background information supported their professional qualifications for the job
- Job candidate's site conveyed a professional image
- Job candidate was well-rounded, showed a wide range of interests
- Job candidate had great communication skills
- Job candidate was creative
- Job candidate received awards and accolades
- Other people posted great references about the job candidate
- Job candidate had interacted with the company's social media accounts
- Job candidate had a large amount of followers or subscribers

ADVANCE PREPARATIONS: YOUR OUTFIT

Several years ago, I was scheduled to give a talk about interviewing skills in a nearby town. On the day of the event it was pouring rain, and as I was racing out the door I grabbed some shoes to change into for my presentation, threw them in a bag, and jumped into the car. In the parking lot, just before my talk, I pulled out the shoes and discovered that I hadn't grabbed a matching pair. This may have gone unnoticed—both shoes were of similar styles and color—but they were both for the left foot! I put them on anyway, headed into the building, and began my talk by telling this story. Then I took off both shoes and gave the rest of my presentation barefoot.

Sharing this experience broke the ice and was a great way to illustrate some of the core aspects of how to physically prepare for an interview. First, choose your shoes before you're rushing out the door! But more importantly, don't fixate on outfit perfection to the point of distraction. Strategizing what to wear in advance of your interview is a key part of making you feel relaxed and prepared for the actual meeting, but if something happens to mar your carefully planned outfit on your way to the meeting—a spill of coffee, for instance, or two left shoes—don't get thrown off by it. Doing something perfectly isn't the most important indicator that you are qualified for a job. How you handle the curveballs that come at you is much more important, and can be compelling for an interviewer—if you got a coffee stain en route, address it with your interviewer at the top of the meeting (and carry a Tide to Go instant stain-remover stick with you; it's been known to work wonders).

But make no mistake, this does not mean that it's fine to have a sloppy appearance. An in-the-moment coffee stain is not the same as a rumpled suit or untidy nails. Pull yourself together, make sure you've got everything you need to bring with you, and dive into the interview day with the confidence that you'll be at your best.

THE BASIC BREAKDOWN

No less than three days before your interview, make the final decisions about your outfit. In corporate America, you have choices about what to wear, but there are still guidelines for appropriate dress. Remember, you want to fit in and appear as if you belong in the company's culture. I've broken down certain rules of thumb by gender in the Dress and Appearance for Men and Women callouts, in order to make things as clear as possible.

Choose something that will convey a polished, professional look, and that communicates your readiness to enter or reenter the professional workforce. Dress one step above what the general attire is for that particular work environment—if the dress code is business casual, wear a suit to the interview. If jeans are the norm, guys should wear khakis and a sport coat, and women should wear a neat dress or skirt or pants with an appropriate top. One caveat here is if the company told you no suit is necessary—then follow the guidelines they set so you don't stand out as not fitting in.

Also, be mindful of the appropriateness of tattoos for the workplace where you're interviewing. If you can cover up the tattoos or downplay them for the interview, do. Pay attention to the cut of your shirt to obscure neck tattoos, and the weight of your shirt to conceal tattoos on the chest and arms—if the material is too thin, tattoos may show through. Women should consider wearing dark stockings or pants to cover up leg and ankle tattoos.

Whatever you choose, be sure that it fits you and is ironed and clean. If any items need to be dry-cleaned, make sure you leave time to get this done. And be sure to wear something that you are physically comfortable in so that your outfit doesn't distract you during the interview.

DRESS AND APPEARANCE FOR MEN

Clothes and Shoes

- Wear a full suit or nice slacks and a coordinating jacket. Suits should be navy blue or black—avoid pinstripes, unless they're very thin and muted.

- Wear a conservatively colored shirt, nothing crazy. A safe bet is to stick with white or pale blue.

- Coordinate your tie with your suit. Splashes of color can be fine, but don't go wild, and don't wear loud patterns. Red is called the power color for a reason—it catches the eye and focuses attention on the wearer. Someone wise once said that a tidy $2 tie is always better than a rumpled $100 tie.

- Wear clean, polished dress shoes, free of dirt and scuff marks. Shiny shoes are for weddings; invest in a pair of non-shiny black, cordovan, or dark-brown shoes. And make sure your socks match your shoes!

Accessories and Jewelry

- Take studs out of visible piercings, and don't wear flashy jewelry.

- Wear a watch, something simple with a leather or metal band—it conveys efficiency and punctuality.

- If you want to wear a flag or ribbon pin on your lapel, be aware that they may initiate conversations that you don't want to have during the interview.

Hair, Nails, and Face

- Facial hair should at the very least be neatly trimmed. Depending on the industry you're pursuing, you may want to shave off your facial hair entirely if it will convey a better fit for the company's culture.

- Make sure nails are trimmed, neat, and clean.

DRESS AND APPEARANCE FOR WOMEN

Clothes and Shoes

- Wear a dress, skirt and jacket, or nice pantsuit with coordinating dress shirt. If you choose a dress or skirt, make sure the length goes at least to your knees. You don't want to be tugging at it or worrying that you're flashing too much skin during the interview.

- Whatever you wear, keep colors simple. It is fine to use something bright as an accent, but don't overdo it—that well-tailored yellow blouse might help you stand out, but you don't want to be remembered as the one in the blaring red pantsuit. If you sweat a lot, avoid silks and light colors.

- Wear closed-toe shoes or boots with a heel, though not a stiletto or platform. Flats are too informal. Whether you are 4'10" or 6'1", you carry yourself more professionally when wearing shoes that keep you on your toes.

- Wear stockings—they convey a more professional look than bare legs. Always pack a spare pair of stockings in your handbag to ensure against last-minute runs.

Accessories and Jewelry

- Choose one statement piece of jewelry and stop there. A distinctive necklace can be a great conversation starter. Stay away from large earrings, as they are distracting.

- If you have multiple piercings in either of your ears, take out all but the primary earrings. If you have visible piercings other than in your ears, remove the studs for the interview. Depending on your ethnicity, nose piercings may be part of your culture, but be aware that they can be distracting for those not accustomed to them.

- If you accent your outfit with a scarf, make sure it's not going to get in your way or give you something to fidget with during the interview.

- Wear a watch; it can be a bracelet watch as long as the watch face is visible—it conveys efficiency and punctuality.

- If you want to wear a flag or ribbon pin, be aware that they may initiate conversations that you don't want to have during the interview.

Hair, Nails, Makeup

- Choose a neat, off-the-face hairstyle. It projects confidence and openness.

- Nails should be groomed, and if you are going to paint them, carefully consider what color to use. This is not the time or place for wild nail art, but if wearing bright polish is part of your personality and won't clash with the company culture, by all means feel free to do so. The safest bet, though, is to choose a neutral shade.

- Wear makeup to convey a professional, put-together look—but don't overdo it. A little goes a long way. Use a bit of mascara, blush, and a dab of lipstick or lip gloss to show that you are appropriately polished. If you, like me, aren't great with makeup, go to the counter at a department store and have them show you how to apply makeup and choose colors that work well for you. Practice applying your look before the morning of the interview.

ADVANCE PREPARATIONS: SUPPLIES

Now that you've sorted out what you're going to wear, you need to gather all other necessary supplies. A successful interview depends on strong supporting materials and the proper preparation as much as it does on the right outfit—it's all about personal presentation.

RÉSUMÉS, BUSINESS CARDS, PEN AND PAPER

Get good-quality paper for your printer and make several copies of your résumé. I am assuming that I do not need to remind you to run spell-check on the document before you hit print! You want to bring several copies of your résumé with you in case more than one person interviews you. And even if you've already sent your résumé to the company, bring copies with you to the interview anyhow. It can be useful for the interviewer to have a copy there in front of him or her to refer to during the interview, and having one ready as soon as you sit down is a great way to communicate organization and preparedness.

Business cards aren't necessary, but they can be a nice touch. You can make them inexpensively through www.vistaprint.com. Pay the extra few dollars to have the Vistaprint logo removed.

You also want to bring pens and a notebook or pad of paper with you to the interview. A simple leather portfolio can be a handy way to carry these items and provides a writing surface for taking notes during the meeting. But make sure your portfolio has a plain cover and is not embossed with the logo of some other company!

BRIEFCASE OR BAG

Choose something professional, and pack it in advance—this gives you time to remember everything you need to put in it. A briefcase or computer bag is fine to use, but a backpack or messenger bag thrown across your body is not. Women have more options than men—a large purse that doubles as a briefcase can be great as long as your portfolio and résumés can be removed from it easily, without putting your personal effects on display. Also, women: If you are going to bring your heels and change into them right before the interview, choose a professional-looking bag that can hold your street shoes during the interview and still give you easy access to your portfolio, notebook, and pens.

REFERENCES

When a company is seriously interested in hiring you, they will usually ask for references, either via a written letter or a brief conversation. Don't wait until this happens to think about who can attest to your skills, capabilities, and leadership style. Strong references can help you clinch a job offer, so choose people who know your talents and skill sets well. Former bosses, coworkers, customers, vendors, and colleagues can all make good references.

New graduates often struggle with references because they don't have a lot of work experience. However, former professors make great references. So do parents from old babysitting jobs and bosses from internships and summer jobs. Even close family friends who work in a similar industry can attest to your qualifications. For those who are changing careers, your best bet is to find someone from the most recent company you worked for—either a boss or a former colleague. Don't worry that someone cannot verify your abilities in a new field; they can corroborate your work ethic, team approach, and relevant attributes.

With a bit of creativity, returning parents can also find wonderful references. For example, if you volunteered at your child's school or did any pro bono work for an organization, ask someone you worked with to speak about specific skills you used that could also transfer to the job you're pursuing. The same goes for anyone you may know through the PTA, charities, and religious groups. And don't hesitate to reach out to a former boss to speak on your behalf. A mom in my community, Faith, recently decided to reenter the workforce after nearly eight years of being Super Mom. She truly was. She coordinated playdates, picked up other people's kids, organized fund-raisers for the school, and served as the head of the parents' committee and as treasurer of the PTA. She also volunteered for one of the main community rebuilding initiatives after Hurricane Sandy. I always said she was one of the hardest-working unpaid people I knew. When she asked for friends to act as references, people were lining up to sing her praises.

References may feel like a greater challenge for those who were fired or laid off. Keep in mind that layoffs are common every time the economy takes a turn. If you were let go for a cause other than layoffs, it is important to understand the reasons for your termination. Still, someone from a previous workplace should be considered for supplying a reference, even if it is a place from which you were laid off or fired. There is often someone still there with whom you worked well. I know that I have personally decided to part ways with employees and still provided references for them when I can speak genuinely to specific strengths they have. If you left your last job on a positive note, even if you were fired, your former boss would be a great reference. I have a friend, Aaron, who fired an employee but still provided a strong reference. He let the employee go because that person was not growing in his role, and it didn't match his interests. Aaron had a frank conversation with him about this, and then helped him with his search. There may very well be people at a former workplace willing to provide references for you, regardless of the circumstances under which you left.

If there is someone who would make a strong reference but might be unavailable during your job search, ask for a letter in advance. Simply tell the potential employer why that person is not directly available. If you are going on an intensive job search and are concerned about giving someone's contact information to too many potential employers, that is another appropriate time to ask for a letter of reference from them to distribute instead of their contact details.

When providing contact information for verbal references, always ask permission of the person you are listing as a reference before giving out his or her details. Also give your references a heads-up when they should be expecting a call, and clarify for them any traits you want them to highlight about you.

QUESTIONS

Based on the job description, you can guess at the questions you will be asked during the interview. Review the common questions listed in Chapter 6 and think through any potential questions. Then ask a friend or family member to run through them with you so you can practice and get some feedback.

At a certain point during the interview, the interviewer will turn the conversation over to you, and *you'll* have the chance to ask the questions. Prepare your questions in advance as much as you possibly can. Even if you don't write them down, think them through. I'll go over what to ask in great detail in Chapter 8.

LAST-MINUTE PREPARATIONS AND TIPS

You've done a great job with advance preparations, planning, and pulling together what you need to ensure that you put your best possible self forward. Once the day of the interview arrives, you should be poised to check the last few things off your list and wrap up loose ends. Here's a quick reference for you to go through before you head out the door. See the Interview-Preparation Checklist in the bonus section for a full list.

- Get a good night's sleep the evening before, and set two alarm clocks just in case.

- Do not skip breakfast! You absolutely must eat something the morning of the interview, but it should be something that sits well in your stomach. Also, do not drink soda or any other carbonated beverage before your interview. No smoking, no chewing tobacco, and no garlic with your eggs. Know your stomach and choose food wisely.

- If you haven't yet tested out the commute, leave plenty of travel time to account for unforeseen traffic.

- Stash a small bottle of water in your bag, which you'll already have packed with your résumés, business cards, pens, and notepaper. If you think you might get hungry, throw a snack in the bag, too.

- Breath mints (not gum) and dental floss also can be indispensable. What's more embarrassing than realizing after the fact that you've had something stuck in your teeth the whole time?

- Learn from my mistake! If you're bringing your dress shoes to change into right before the interview, make sure you have a matching pair.

- Ladies, don't forget your lipstick or lip gloss, whichever you're using. After applying lipstick, put your finger in your mouth and then pull it out to remove any excess that might smudge your teeth. Do this again right before the interview starts.

- Men, do a second check in the mirror to make sure any nose or ear hairs are trimmed.

- Once you've gotten dressed, remove all keys and jingling change from your pockets. If you tend to twist rings while they are on your fingers (newly married men, I am talking especially to you), leave them at home.

- On the topic of perfume and cologne, the answer is: absolutely not. You are often in a small, enclosed space during an interview, and the scents from perfume and cologne can become overpowering. And if you are interviewing with someone pregnant, I can tell you from firsthand experience that strong perfume and cologne scents can make your mother-to-be interviewer dizzy and nauseated—not exactly the first impression you want to make.

- Hit the facilities before heading into the interview. You don't want to be sitting there, in the middle of an important discussion, thinking about how much you need to rush off to the restroom.

Now that you've done everything you can to prepare fully for the interview, all you can do is get there and wait for it to begin. In Chapter 3, we'll look at how to make the most of this in-between time before your interview begins.

REFRESH YOUR MEMORY

- Appearances matter. How you present yourself speaks volumes about your attitude and indicates how you will represent and reflect on the company if you're hired. Be pressed, polished, and prepared.

- Also manage your online presence to project the most positive impression possible.

- No less than three days before your interview, make the final decisions about your outfit. Go through the above checklists to sort out what you'll wear to represent you at your best and most relaxed and confident.

- Gather all other necessary supplies: résumé, business cards, references, and your question list. A successful interview depends on strong supporting materials as much as it does on the right outfit—it's all about personal presentation.

- Get a good night's sleep before the interview, eat a solid breakfast that will sit well in your stomach, and leave plenty of time to get to your meeting.

- Before you walk out the door, run through the above reference guide step-by-step to ensure that everything is in place and you're ready to go.

THE INTERVIEW DAY

CHAPTER 3:
WORK IT WHILE YOU WAIT

MANAGING YOUR TIMING, NERVES, AND THE WAITING ROOM

You look great, you left your house early, and now you're out the door and on your way to the interview. Questions may be racing through your mind as you head to your meeting. How early should you arrive? What do you do to keep yourself calm while you're sitting in the waiting room? How do you maintain the mental clarity and focus you worked so hard to attain while preparing? Regardless of your age, gender, or background, there are some basic tips to help you navigate any jitters that can strike during the commute and waiting room moments.

TIMING IT RIGHT

Times have changed and there are increased security measures in many buildings these days. It has gotten tricky to figure out exactly how much time to give yourself to clear security when arriving at a building for the first time, but the rule of thumb is simple: *Err on the side of caution.* Assume that you will need to wait in line before getting your security tag and that you may need to have your bag searched. In larger buildings, there are often bag-scanning machines and metal detectors similar to those at airports. Do not let your timing go down to the wire—that's one sure way to shatter your mental calmness before the interview has even begun. Leave yourself plenty of time to get through any security measures.

Once you've cleared security—and, if necessary, changed into your interview shoes—check your watch. If you've got more than 15 minutes to go until your appointment, hang out in the lobby for a little while. Fifteen minutes is the maximum amount of time that you want to arrive before an interview. On the other hand, showing up five minutes before an interview is as late as you want to be. Anything between these two guideposts is perfect for showing timeliness but not pressuring the interviewer to wrap up his or her work because you are waiting. You also don't want to give yourself too much time to busy yourself and let your nerves take over while you're waiting.

THE WAITING GAME

As someone who is habitually early, I often find myself with time on my hands in the waiting room. I've learned to use this as an opportunity to increase my preparedness, get a feel for the company's culture, and manage my nerves.

The first thing to do is greet the receptionist in a friendly and respectful manner. Never, ever treat the receptionist (or anybody) with condescension, regardless of the level of the position you are seeking. You are not looking to impress just those employees whom you deem your superiors. Every person at every level of an organization counts, and the attitudes you display are core indicators of your suitability to a company's culture.

At one company where I used to work, our firm had the great policy of seeking input from the receptionist when evaluating interview candidates. There was one extremely qualified and promising candidate who treated the receptionist as if she were below him—and her feedback afterward was the main reason he didn't get the job. From the moment you walk through the door at a potential workplace, you are being evaluated; treat everyone—*everyone*—as you would like to be treated, with dignity and respect. I'll often chat with the receptionist because it puts me at ease and connects me with my personable side right before I'm meeting an interviewer.

Another suggestion: Go to the restroom once you've arrived at the office but before your interview is scheduled to begin. It gives you a few minutes to check your appearance and make sure you're physically prepared.

While seated in the waiting room, see if there are any materials to read. Often a company will set out its annual reports or an array of newspapers or magazines it deems relevant to its business. Scanning these will distract you from any possible jitters and may provide you with interesting conversation points and questions for the interview.

In this day and age, most of us are guilty of checking our phones when we have a few spare minutes. This is fine to do quickly while you're waiting, but I suggest you avoid it entirely. You can easily get caught up reading or responding to absorbing emails or texts, which can distract you, especially if you've received upsetting news. For parents, make sure your kids' school or your sitter has alternative numbers to call in case of an emergency, so you'll be able to turn off your phone without fearing you're missing an important call. If you're leaving your phone on, at the very least switch your ringer to silent mode. And don't check your watch or the clock every two minutes. Not only will you lose focus, but you will also elevate your anxiety level. You want to remain fully in the present during the moments just before the interview is set to start.

CALMING YOUR NERVES

Think about how nerves manifest for you. Are you a sweater? A fidgeter? Does your voice get shaky or do you obsessively click your pen? There are actionable steps you can take to calm yourself down and ensure that your nerves don't get the best of you. The fact is that almost all physical manifestations of nerves are brought about by your mind. So the name of the game is to calm your mind.

The first thing you must realize and remind yourself of is that interviewers aren't out to get you. They want to learn about you and assess whether or not you're the right fit for the job. And in fact the same is true for you. Yes, you want a job, but you also want to find the *right* job for *you*. Remember that as the interviewee you too are in a position of strength. You are bringing your expertise and experience to the situation and have the potential to elevate the organization. *That* is the mind-set that will help you squash those pesky nerves.

Below are some more techniques to help you manage the specific effects nerves may have on you. I have divided the tips into three categories: mental, behavioral, and physical.

MENTAL TECHNIQUES

Mental messages truly control the effects of nerves. Use these techniques to get yourself into the right frame of mind.

- **Remember your three words.** Take the last few moments before an interview to remind yourself of the three words you chose in Chapter 1 to best represent you. Clear your mind and focus on them. Believe them. Be them.

- **See it in your mind's eye.** Visualize yourself in the interview feeling relaxed and natural. Imagine seeing the face of the interviewer, engaged and interested in what you have to say.

- **Affirm and self-credit.** Remind yourself of what you do well, and give yourself credit for your knowledge. Remember what first drew you to this position and how your skill sets demonstrate your suitability.

- **Project confidence.** To manage self-doubt, think about what confidence looks like in your facial expression, eye contact, and stance, and what it sounds like in your voice. Then practice these things and let muscle memory take over. If you don't believe in you, you make it much harder for anyone else to believe in you.

BEHAVIORAL TECHNIQUES

The following ideas will help you frame your actions and project confidence, even when you are not 100 percent feeling it.

- **Don't let them see you sweat.** If you sweat when you get nervous, or even think you might sweat if you're nervous, leave on your sport coat or wear a blazer so that you don't have to worry about unsightly sweat patches on your shirt or blouse. Before the interview, you may want to pop into the restroom to dab cool water on the insides of your wrists and behind your ears to cool yourself down.

- **Be prepared.** Spend a few moments thinking through the questions the interviewer may ask you and how your experiences reflect your suitability. Before the day of the interview, ask a friend to do a mock interview with you to get some feedback on your answers, then reflect on this constructive preparation while you're in the waiting room.

- **Counter the nerves.** Sometimes feeling the effects of nerves and getting self-conscious about them only amplifies their effects. If your excess energy makes you fidget or shake, use your time in the waiting room to do some simple exercises that will diffuse your adrenaline and calm your mind. Squeeze and release your hands, stretch your legs and toes, clear your throat, chat with someone else in the room, or drink a glass of warm water to steady your voice.

- **Act as if you believe.** You've heard the phrase "Fake it until you make it"? Well, make this work for you. Think about how an authentically confident, competent candidate carries him or herself, and then visualize yourself being this candidate. If you show the interviewer what a dynamic, engaging interviewee looks like, that is what you will be.

- **Laugh it off.** If you tend to get clumsy when you're nervous, the most useful thing you can do is to not make a big deal of it. Imagine yourself dropping your pen or stumbling a bit when first walking into the interview room, and then imagine letting yourself laugh about it and not acting too concerned. Realize that you set the tone for how someone reacts to your minor stumble. If you are OK with a slipup, the interviewer will be OK with it, too. Recovering gracefully can project your confidence and actually work to your advantage. Although please don't plan to trip yourself up on purpose!

PHYSICAL TECHNIQUES

Everyone has his or her own unique physical and physiological responses to anxiety. One common one, blushing, occurs when the tiniest blood vessels in your face, the capillaries, suddenly get wider. Your blood vessels widen in response to signals sent by the brain through the nerves.[1] And when they widen, more blood flows through them, giving your skin a reddened, rosy appearance.

Below are suggestions to counter common physical effects of the nerves. Some of the physical techniques for countering nerves overlap with the behavioral techniques above because our behaviors are often physical responses to the onset of nerves.

Sweating

- Wear dark clothing

- Bring a handkerchief to discreetly wipe your brow or hands

- Use cornstarch, liquid talc, or baby powder to counter the sweats. Apply it when getting dressed and bring a small bottle with you to refresh yourself right before the interview if need be.

- Keep your hands on your lap, where sweat can be absorbed by your pants or skirt fabric, until getting up from your seat

---

1   www.askdoctork.com/what-causes-blushing-20111226927

Dry Mouth

- Drink a glass of room-temperature water

- Bite your tongue

- Suck on a lozenge

- Imagine eating a lemon

Shaking Voice

- Clear your throat

- Project your voice as you start speaking; stretching your vocal cords eases the shakes.

- Yawn while you're in the waiting room (don't do this once in the interview!)

- Wiggle your jaw

- Do breathing exercises such as inhaling slowly as you count to four and exhaling for the same four count. This also helps with slowing your heart rate.

- Drink a glass of water slowly

Shaking Hands or Legs

- Clench and then unclench the muscles in the area of the body that shakes

- Pull up or push down on the chair you are sitting on

- Press your palms together

- Wiggle or crunch your toes

- Do not cross your legs while sitting; you may get pins and needles when you stand up or start bopping your leg.

Blushing

- Look up instead of down

- Use the mental techniques above to focus on calming your nerves

- Control breathing, relax muscles, calm your mind

One thing to remember is that no matter how confident you are, you will never completely eliminate your nerves—and you shouldn't. Nerves let you know that you care about something. They keep energy in your body. Your job is simply to get all your butterflies flying in the same direction and put that adrenaline to work for you.

REFRESH YOUR MEMORY

- Leave yourself time to clear security once you've reached the building.

- You want to arrive at the interview 5 to 15 minutes before your appointment—if you're earlier than this, wait in the lobby for a bit before proceeding to the interview.

- Once you're in the waiting room, greet everyone you encounter with respect, including the receptionist. The attitudes you display indicate your professionalism and suitability for the company's culture.

- Go to the restroom before your interview begins to do one last check on your appearance.

- Leave your phone alone if you can, and whatever you do, silence the ringer!

- Calm your nerves. Remember your three words, visualize yourself feeling relaxed and confident in the interview, and remind yourself of your strengths and qualifications.

- If your nerves manifest themselves physically, manage any tendency to sweat, ease the fidgets with simple muscle exercises, and drink a glass of room-temperature water to counter dry mouth.

STAGE I
RAPPORT BUILDING

CHAPTER 4:
BUILD AN INSTANT RAPPORT

CREATING A POSITIVE IMPRESSION AND
THE POWER OF SMALL TALK

You're still sitting in the waiting room, lobby, or receptionist's area when finally you notice that an employee is walking directly toward you, and you realize that this must be the person who is going to interview you. What should you do? I always hope that an interviewer will find me chatting with someone to immediately show that I am personable. One thing you should definitely *not* do if you've caught his or her eye is look nervously away. First encounters are extremely important, and you want to create a positive impression from the very beginning.

Before we dive into the actual interview, let's quickly review its five basic stages. All the stages build upon one another, and they are all key to the process, even if many of them are brief.

The stages are:

1. **Rapport Building:** (Chapter 4) The initial greeting is made, and the general tone for the interview is set.

2. **Opening Questions:** (Chapter 5) The interviewer usually starts with a few easy questions to increase the comfort level of the situation and establish an overview of your personality and experiences.

3. **Core:** (Chapters 6 and 7) This is the most substantive part of the process. The interviewer gathers critical information, asks deeper questions, seeks contrary information, and continues assessing your compatibility with the position and the company's culture.

4. **Candidate Q&A:** (Chapter 8) You get to ask the interviewer the questions *you* have and reemphasize what is important to you.

5. **Closing:** (Chapter 9) This is your last chance to make sure that the interviewer knows everything about you that he or she should know. Create a positive, lasting impression and find out what's involved in next steps, the timing of the hire decision, and how best to follow up.

Early in my career, I landed an interview with Disney, which I was thrilled about. But when I arrived for the interview, the interviewer had me sit on an enormous couch. I'm 4'10", and I felt like an Oompa Loompa as the couch seemed to swallow me whole. I sat stiffly on the edge and couldn't get comfortable, which left me feeling awkward and self-conscious. I realized long after I didn't get the second interview that my being ill at ease left the interviewer feeling the exact same way.

The fact is that we are always communicating, often without saying a word. My body language on the couch was speaking volumes about how I was uncomfortably faking it all through the interview—in other words, I was playing charades, and it showed.

The goal during the first few moments of an interview is to create a relaxed environment that will let you shine. Remember, you may not be the only one feeling awkward and nervous. This is the first time the interviewer is meeting you as well, and he or she may also need a moment to settle into the rhythm of the interview. Unless you're speaking with someone from human resources (HR), interviewing may not be a regular part of your interviewer's job. If you can help set the tone by putting you both at ease, you'll lay the groundwork for open communication and a successful exchange. Let's take a closer look at how to make a positive first impression and build a lasting rapport.

THE HALO EFFECT

The initial moments of an interview are all about assessing fit. Often unconsciously and before even discussing your experience and skills, an interviewer will be trying to determine if you have a "feel" that could work well for the position. He or she will be picking up on the personality signals you project. How do you carry yourself? How well would you align with the company's culture?

You want the interviewer to be internally saying yes right off the bat. Building rapport sets the tone and often impacts the types of questions you will be asked. Because everyone likes to be correct, if the first impression the interviewer has of you is positive, he or she will seek to prove that instinct right throughout the rest of the interview. The interviewer may even be more inclined to ask you questions that allow you to highlight strengths and shine, and to help you out if you get tripped up.

In short, people like to trust their first impressions. This phenomenon is often referred to as the halo effect: feeling generally good or bad about a candidate based on one thing heard or observed early during the interview, which then colors the evaluation of all the candidate's other attributes. If you establish a good rapport in the initial moments, chances are that your interviewer will carry this positive impression of you throughout the course of your meeting. Likewise, if you do something jarring or inappropriate that creates a negative first impression, this is the instinct that the interviewer will be inclined to trust, and you will have to work extra hard to reset the halo. The first five minutes of an interview are crucial for strengthening positive rapport.

So how exactly do you go about doing this?

BE PREPARED FOR THE MEET AND GREET

Don't let your initial encounter take you off guard. As you're in the waiting room, you know that you are going to meet the person who will be interviewing you at any moment. Carry things in your left hand and always leave your right arm free—an unencumbered right arm allows you to easily extend your hand for a handshake as soon as the interviewer approaches. If there is a coatroom available, take advantage of this when you first arrive so that you'll be less encumbered. If this isn't an option, have your coat draped over your left arm. If your bag or briefcase is on the floor, be sure that this, too, is on your left. That way, after the initial greeting, you can quickly pick up the bag and be on your way without the interviewer having to wait.

You may not know in advance who your interviewer will be. Whether the interviewer is the same gender as you or not, treat the person with respect and courtesy. I have opened doors for men as well as women, and appreciate when the same is done for me. I'll always offer to help carry something if a person is burdened with papers or bags, and you should do the same—it is simply polite.

You always want to project confidence. Don't let your demeanor be overly eager, but also don't feel the need to be too stiff and formal. In the corporate world, respect is often conveyed through a warm cordiality. Confidence comes from the voice, stance, handshake, eye contact, and smile. These last few minutes you've spent waiting for the interview to begin should have given you the chance to get into a calm, confident mind-set. Project this as you establish eye contact with the interviewer, smile in a warm and natural way, and rise from your chair to greet him or her. People want to be comfortable and connect with their colleagues. Put the interviewer at ease from the get-go and show that you are open to establishing a good connection.

COMMUNICATE CLEARLY WITH YOUR NONVERBAL SIGNALS

What we communicate without words is just as important as what we say with them throughout the interview, but this is especially true at the beginning. Social psychologist and Harvard Professor Amy Cuddy's research focuses on how nonverbal expressions of power—with the body expansive and the limbs stretched out—affect people's feelings, behaviors, and hormone levels. In particular, her research shows that "faking" body postures associated with dominance and power ("power posing")—even for as little as two minutes—increases people's testosterone, decreases their cortisol, increases their appetite for risk, and causes them to perform better in job interviews. In my words, you can trick your mind through your body, and it results in a profound effect on how a person feels. There are several actionable steps you can take to be sure your nonverbal messages are enhancing the positive impression you make as the interview begins.

KNOW THE POWER OF A GREAT HANDSHAKE

I recently met with a new acquaintance and commented on his good handshake. He told me that he immediately judged people by their handshakes and was almost always right about these impressions. Although I would hope that people would gather more information about someone before judging him or her, it is true that it can be easy to make assumptions about people based on their handshakes. If a handshake is too weak, it suggests that the person lacks confidence. If it is too strong, it might be a sign that the person is overcompensating or trying to intimidate.

The handshake is a critical nonverbal gesture and conveys a wealth of information within the first few moments of an interaction. Whatever your experience level, it is completely acceptable to initiate a handshake: It projects that you are confident and comfortable with the interaction. Go ahead and be the first to offer your hand.

When you shake hands with someone, make sure you're giving what I call a "web" handshake—the web of your hand, between your thumb and forefinger, should touch the web of the other person's hand. You want to clasp the other hand firmly—don't grasp the fingertips and give a limp shake, but don't crush the hand in yours either, and don't pump the arm up and down. You simply need to clasp the hand with confidence, and shake it in an efficient yet friendly greeting. Combine the firm handshake with direct eye contact and a warm smile.

If you're unsure what it's like to execute a good handshake, practice in advance of your interview. A solid handshake will immediately communicate that you are relaxed and open, helping to create a positive impression upon the interviewer.

TAKE A SEAT—THE RIGHT WAY

Yes, there is a right way to sit for an interview, which means there's a wrong way, too, as I learned during my Disney interview debacle. Do it correctly from the very beginning to amplify your comfort, mobility, and approachability.

You don't want to sit all the way back in the chair. Find a comfortable position slightly forward on the seat. If you are height challenged, like me, sitting on the front part of the chair enables both feet to be firmly planted on the floor. More importantly, this position keeps your body energized, not passive. If you can lean forward you will be able to express animation and engagement through movements and gestures. If you are seated too far back in your chair, you risk being engulfed by it and sapped of your natural energy.

You want to have control over your body not just to enable movement but also to project the enthusiastic image of your three words. If it will help, feel free to sit at an angle. Again, you don't want to be too stiff and formal, so find a position that feels natural and comfortable but not excessively casual. If it takes you a few seconds to get comfortable, don't be self-conscious about this; it's better to disarm the situation with a quick joke about getting comfy than it is to suffer in discomfort and awkwardness for the entire interview. It is critical that you are confident, alert, *and* comfortable throughout the interview, and the opening moments are exactly the time to establish these attitudes and communicate them to your interviewer.

If you are seated at a table, leave a bit of space between yourself and the table. You want to be able to lean forward to take notes on the table if necessary, but you also want to have some room so that you can use your hands to emphasize what you're saying, and to shift your position if necessary so that you can fully engage and display your energy.

SIT UP STRAIGHT, USE YOUR HANDS, AND SMILE

After I give a talk, people are often surprised to realize my petite size because I, as they put it, "appear taller." The key to doing this is to take up your space. I imagine a marionette string going up my spine and being pulled taut. Good posture absolutely conveys confidence and openness. Remember this as you are taking your seat for the interview, and roll back your shoulders to broaden the width of your chest, which will immediately improve your posture and communicate that you feel sure of yourself and at ease.

Open shoulders also facilitate wider hand motions. Rather than just utilizing the narrow space in front of your body, use your hands to punctuate what you are saying and convey meaning as you speak. But don't overdo it, and be careful not to fidget or do something repetitive and distracting such as clicking a pen or twisting your wedding band. For some, using your hands may take getting used to, so practice in your everyday conversations.

Remember to maintain an open, alert expression, and to smile. Smiling is something many of us do naturally, but if it isn't it can work against you in the professional world. I was recently talking to a bank hiring manager who had just interviewed a candidate for a position but ultimately didn't offer him the job because he hadn't smiled once or exuded any warmth or personality during the interview. The position would have required interacting with customers on a regular basis, and while the hiring manager conceded that the man may have been capable of a friendly demeanor, he hadn't exhibited that during the interview.

You want your smile to be genuine, not plastered on and fake, but you can convey the energy of a smile without constantly grinning from ear to ear. Nodding or tilting your head in agreement and expressing curiosity and interest with your eyes are additional ways to show that you are present and engaged. You want to communicate to the interviewer that you are listening and responsive, that you are enjoying the dialogue that the two of you are having, and that this is the attitude you will have in the workplace if hired.

EYE CONTACT IS KEY

Direct eye contact may be considered a sign of aggression or disrespect in some countries. However, in professional environments in the United States, eye contact is a sign of self-confidence and indicates interest in the conversation and the speaker. It connects you to those with whom you're speaking and enables you to read their reactions, an important aspect of the interviewing process.

Eye contact should be direct, not superficial. Aim to sustain eye contact for the length of a complete sentence. Most importantly, do what feels natural. If you find it a challenge to maintain direct eye contact, look between the interviewer's eyebrows or at the bridge of his or her nose. Avoid darting, robotic eye movements. If you feel that you're staring too intensely, loosen your focus so that you're looking in the direction of the interviewer for a few moments but perhaps not staring directly into his or her eyes.

When thinking or answering questions, it is OK to look away in thought, but be aware of how you may be doing it—studies show that when you look up it indicates that you are thinking, but when you look down it often indicates a lack of confidence. Show with facial animation that you are processing the thought rather than registering a blank or lost expression. If you've looked away while you're thinking, reestablish eye contact before answering. If there is more than one person in the room, include everyone with your eyes when answering a question.

FOLLOW THEIR LEAD

The best interviews are two-sided conversations full of verbal and nonverbal messages. Just as the interviewer is assessing your signals, you should be picking up on his or her signals as well. Watch the interviewer's body language and take your rapport-building cues from this. Does the interviewer smile in a relaxed and welcoming way as you're being seated? If so, a few minutes of on-topic but light-hearted small talk could help transition into the core of the interview. Does the interviewer seem more focused on immediately getting down to business? If so, follow that lead. A key part of what the interviewer is assessing in these first few moments is how well you read and respond to a situation. Communicate your ability to navigate this well by taking your cues from the signals the interviewer is sending.

MATCH THEIR LANGUAGE AND WATCH YOUR JARGON

When you travel to a foreign country, it helps if you know a little of the local language. Entering a new company or industry is similar in many ways. You must learn the customs, culture, and language of the landscape to fit in. An interview is the perfect time to hone and demonstrate those skills.

One question that often arises is the level of formality you should use in your language and mannerisms. Keep in mind, the norm in corporate America is what I call cordial casual. However, if you are a new grad, your definition of casual may be too casual. Most people address their colleagues at all levels of an organization by first name. But if you are uncertain about how to address your interviewer, it is OK to use Mr. or Ms. at first and wait until the interviewer invites you to call him or her by first name. By the same token, maintain a level of friendly respect with your language. Even if an interviewer curses during your conversation, it is inappropriate for you to do so.

Something that everyone, especially the career changer, needs to be aware of is the use of jargon. We all adopt a slang or shorthand vocabulary that doesn't translate across industries, and often it isn't decipherable outside an individual company. You never want your interviewer to be unsure about what you are saying or make him or her feel dumb by having to ask. If you have been out of an industry for some time, be careful not to throw around lingo that might date you. Match the wording and phrasing used by the organization you're interviewing with. If an interviewer uses jargon you are unfamiliar with during your meeting, it is OK to ask what it stands for. It may even be an appropriate moment to use humor, remarking that each company and industry seems to have its own lingo. You don't have to become an expert on the language of the industry you're interviewing in before you land the job; simply avoid introducing any confusion about how prepared you are to enter or reenter the industry.

SMALL TALK LEADS TO BIGGER CONVERSATION

Small talk does not have to be meaningless. It can create commonalities and build connections. You want to show your comfort, confidence, and personality. If your interviewer starts off the meeting with some small talk, follow that lead.

There are standby small talk topics that we all use every day to connect with the people we encounter. A news item that is not too politically charged, for instance, or, yes, even the weather may be the perfect way to ease into a conversation and break the ice. If you experienced something interesting on your way to the office, or noticed something particularly noteworthy while in the lobby, take the opportunity to remark upon this. A funny story or an innocuous joke can display your personality. Look around you—are there pictures on the walls or knickknacks on the desk that catch your eye? Build a positive, relaxed rapport by commenting on the things at hand.

Avoid introducing hot-button topics like religion or politics during the interview, especially right at the beginning. Also, don't spend the whole interview talking about your kids. You may pick up on a child's artwork or a family picture hanging on a wall, which can be a natural conversation starter, especially for parents. As a mom myself, I could talk about my kids all day long, but it's not really appropriate at this stage of the job hunt. Also, you should know that legally you do not have to disclose that you have children. It is illegal for an interviewer to ask you if you have children or evaluate your candidacy based upon personal criteria such as parenthood. It is at your discretion whether or not you want to use that information to create a connection with the interviewer. You may see the interviewer become uncomfortable if you introduce the topic, since it's not a normal part of an interview conversation. If that happens, again, follow the interviewer's lead.

Understand the value of small talk in laying the foundation for the larger conversation. If you establish a positive rapport with your interviewer and help create an environment in which you both feel at ease, the rest of the conversation will flow more naturally and allow you to spotlight the real and best you.

Mastering the above components will help you make an excellent first impression on the interviewer. And as we all know—thanks to the halo effect—it is much easier to make a good first impression than to change a bad one. Incorporate these concepts into the beginning of your meeting and you'll be well poised to handle the next stage of the interview: the introductory question.

REFRESH YOUR MEMORY

- Know the five stages of an interview. They build upon one another and are all critically important, even if many of them are brief.

- We are always communicating, often without saying a word. Use both verbal and nonverbal language to establish a good rapport and create a positive impression from the get-go.

- Remember the halo effect: If the interviewer has an initial positive impression of you, that is the idea he or she is likely to maintain throughout the course of the interview. A strong impression will set the interview off on the right foot.

- Be prepared for the meet and greet by having your right hand free to extend in a handshake and your personal belongings efficiently organized at your left side.

- Master the elements of a good handshake, connecting the "web" of your hand with that of the other person and giving a firm, efficient, friendly shake.

- Sit on the front part of your seat, with your posture straight but your face and shoulders open and relaxed.

- Use your hands to punctuate what you are saying and convey meaning as you speak, but don't overdo it with fidgeting or nervous gestures.

- Smile! Communicate a warm personality and readiness to engage with a genuine smile, and nod when appropriate to indicate agreement and interest.

- Direct eye contact is key—it connects you to those with whom you're speaking and enables you to read their reactions.

- Watch the interviewer's body language and listen to what he or she is saying, and take your rapport-building cues from this. A key part of what the interviewer is assessing is how well you read and respond to a situation. Match the interviewer's language, avoid using jargon, and don't be afraid to initiate small talk if the interviewer indicates a willingness to chat to ease into the conversation.

STAGE II
THE INTRODUCTORY QUESTION

CHAPTER 5:
EXCEL AT THE OPENING QUESTIONS

CONNECTING THE DOTS BETWEEN
PAST WORK EXPERIENCES

You're in the office and have been establishing a positive rapport with the interviewer, so you've successfully accomplished the first stage of the interview. Now the interview conversation begins in earnest. The opening questions—and more importantly, how you answer them—give you the chance to begin detailing your qualifications and serve as the transition to the heart of the interview. In this chapter we'll take a closer look at how to excel at the opening questions. In the chapters that follow we'll examine how to handle the core part of the interview, your opportunity to ask questions of the interviewer, and the best way to wrap things up.

ACE THE OPENING QUESTIONS

The progression of the five interview stages creates an opportunity for open but structured dialogue. After establishing an initial rapport, the opening questions are like a bridge that helps the conversation move into the core of the interview. Use this arc to your advantage.

With the first few questions, the interviewer is still getting to know you and establishing groundwork. Two of the most common opening queries are, "Tell me about yourself" and "Walk me through your résumé." Some candidates loathe these questions, as they are broad and it falls upon the candidate to structure responses and lead the conversation. But this is precisely why they should be your favorite questions. Opening questions give you the chance to tell the interviewer exactly what you want him or her to know—*you* get to set the tone.

If you have done your homework and understand in advance what the desirable criteria are for the role—and how they align with your qualifications—then you will be able to provide the interviewer with the key answers and information that he or she needs. We will more fully examine the different types of core interview questions and how to be prepared with structured responses in Chapter 6, but first let's take a look at how to successfully answer those two most common opening questions.

"TELL ME ABOUT YOURSELF"

I particularly love this query because it's an open invitation to spotlight the primary things you want to be sure you convey. Think about this question as an opportunity to present a personal and professional summary of yourself. What were your previous positions, and what skill sets did these experiences give you? As a new grad, you can share your area of academic focus and your activities outside the classroom. If you are reentering the workforce after time off, use adjectives and descriptions that highlight your skills, and weave in references to any relevant experiences, either paid or unpaid. Those who are changing careers can share what they are passionate about and what has inspired this desire for change. Coaching a sports team, volunteering for the PTA, freelancing, undertaking an internship—all of these are examples of different interests and activities that could support your candidacy.

Answer the "Tell me about yourself" question succinctly but with enough detail that you underscore exactly why you are qualified for the job. This is not the stage for an involved response—there will be time for that in a bit. For the moment, keep your answer to less than two minutes. Your response should introduce the experiences and qualities you possess and want to impress upon the interviewer. This will lay the foundation for the interviewer to ask follow-up questions that will give you the chance to fill in the details.

The "Tell me about yourself" query allows you to steer the conversation in any number of directions, with responses such as "I'm an experienced (fill in the blank)," or "I've really thought about what strengths characterize me best, and they are (fill in the blank)." You may want to focus on specific situations and how they have shaped you in positive and relevant ways, or you may want to talk about your key traits and strengths in a broader context. Either approach is effective; it just depends on what it is precisely that you want to highlight.

The question also makes room for your personality to come through, which will increase your comfort level and may further deepen the connection you've been building with the interviewer. It's entirely appropriate to share details or anecdotes from your personal life if they will showcase your strengths as a candidate. I once spent an entire interview talking about poetry and animals and walked out with an offer in hand. Don't forget to smile and think of the interview process as a conversation rather than a presentation. Relax your language as well as your body.

If you are a returning parent or currently out of work for another reason, don't hide your status. Owning your situation and being able to share your circumstances without apology positions you as comfortable and confident. You are coming from a position of strength rather than weakness. It may sound like spin, but an interview is about marketing yourself and putting your best foot forward. Never lie; just share the best story.

Wrap up your response to the opening question with a sentence that links together the skills, experiences, and interests you've been highlighting and explains how they've led you to pursuing this particular position.

"WALK ME THROUGH YOUR RÉSUMÉ"

Be prepared to walk the interviewer through your résumé in about one to two minutes, spotlighting standout elements and connecting the dots between your experiences. Think of it like you are telling the interviewer a story about your previous work history. Add some details as you go through it, but be selective—you don't want to bog down the interview with irrelevant information, but you do want to provide a clear overview of your experience. Explain what you learned from each role and how these things have contributed to your professional growth. You can either relate this chronologically, showing how the experiences built upon one another, or you can structure your answer around specific skills, detailing how the positions have helped you develop in different areas.

It might be easier for new grads to talk about their work experience chronologically, but if you choose to highlight specific skills, you can tie your key points to areas such as course selection at college, internships, and extracurricular activities. New grads might choose to share why they chose their field of study and any internships they pursued—whether or not these relate directly to the job being pursued, they highlight the skills and knowledge gained during those experiences.

If there are gaps in your résumé, don't panic. This often comes into play with parents returning to work, and also for those who have been fired or laid off. It's best to address the gap honestly and then steer the conversation toward highlighting your skills. You can also share anything you may have done to maintain your skills during your time off. Include any course work you've completed since your last employment, any professional certifications you've earned, or any freelance opportunities you've been involved with. If you were fired, honestly and briefly explain the reason you were let go and explain what you have done to address the issue. You may even be able to leverage that negative experience to show how you have grown from it and how it has made you a better employee and more suited for this particular job. No matter what, never talk bad about a former employer. It's unprofessional and not well received by potential new employers.

Spotlight any of your community involvement. For example, in an interview, a parent returning to work might explain how she or he stopped working to focus on the kids when they were little, then say something like, "But now my youngest is in school full time, and I'm excited to get back to work," and explain any responsibilities undertaken with the PTA or other volunteer projects, or any classes taken. Don't apologize for your work hiatus; it could make you seem less confident. And don't worry about the length of time between employment—remember, you want to find the right job, not just any job, and that takes time.

We'll look closely at how to handle such potential land mines as work-history gaps in Chapter 7, but for now remember that an interviewer will be assessing your ability to respond in a clear, concise, and relevant way as much as he or she will be assessing your specific experiences.

USE "I"

There are many times in your life where sharing the credit and using "we" instead of "I" is a good idea—the interview is not one of them. I see this happen particularly frequently with new grads and returning moms.

If you're a new grad, you may have become accustomed to a team mentality, whether through clubs, sports, fraternities, or group projects. Perhaps it is even difficult at times to identify your specific contribution to a group effort. But it is critical to think about this so that you can confidently speak to the impact you have had. Remember, the company is only hiring you.

The tendency to minimize yourself is something that is often taken on more readily by women than men. To this day, women are taught to be humble and modest and to not overstate. But these qualities will not serve you well during an interview. There is a difference between bragging and confidently sharing and owning your story—don't be shy about taking credit for all you do.

Whether you are relating a story or detailing your experiences, it is crucial to use "I"—it highlights that the stories and experiences are uniquely yours and underscores why they qualify *you* for the job. This is absolutely imperative during an interview.

AND USE YOUR THREE WORDS

Last, but definitely not least, don't forget to use your three words! Responding to an opening question is the perfect chance to incorporate the three words you've determined best characterize you and what you want to project. By introducing these words now, you'll establish them as part of the broader interview conversation, and plant them in the interviewer's mind.

REFRESH YOUR MEMORY

- The opening questions of an interview form a bridge between the initial greeting and the core of the conversation. Although they may seem like softball questions, they are actually an enormous opportunity— they give you the chance to tell the interviewer exactly what you want him or her to know and allow you to set the tone. Use this to your advantage.

- Do your research. Understand as much as possible about the company and the job for which you're applying. Identify the desirable criteria for a well-qualified candidate, then use the opening questions to provide the interviewer with key information that illustrates your suitability for the role.

- Approach the "walk me through your résumé" query as if you're telling a succinct but compelling story about your previous experiences—the highlights of your career, how one dot connects to another, what your academic, volunteer, or community service experiences have been like.

- It is imperative that you use "I" instead of "we" when discussing your experiences during an interview.

- Don't forget to use your three words! Opening questions are the perfect chance to incorporate the three words you've determined best characterize you and further impress them upon the interviewer.

STAGE III
THE INTERVIEW CORE

CHAPTER 6:
PREPARE FOR THE CORE QUESTIONS

INTERVIEW STYLES, STRUCTURED RESPONSES, AND QUESTION TYPES

Once you've moved through the opening questions, you've arrived at the core of the interview. This is when the interviewer will be posing specific questions to determine three basic things:

1. Can you do this job?

2. Do you want to do this job?

3. Will you be a good fit for the company?

This last one, "Will you be a good fit for the company?" is an intuitive element that is really best assessed as the interaction is taking place and will evolve over the course of the interview. The most important thing to do to address it is to be authentic. If you are not yourself, then neither you nor the interviewer will be able to determine if the position is truly right for you. And the fit absolutely needs to be right in order for you to do your best work.

"Do you want to do this job?" will have less relevance in the core part of a first interview. The interviewer will definitely be trying to gauge your genuine enthusiasm for the position, and you should be quite clear about expressing it, as a strong sense in the opposite direction can eliminate your candidacy. However, I always say the first interview is about them deciding if they want you, and the second is about you deciding if you want them—though both sides of the evaluation are always happening in every round.

The first element—"Can you do this job?"—is the one that your interviewer will be focused on most closely during the first interview. He or she will ask specific questions to gather information about your qualifications and compatibility for the position. With every answer you give, the interviewer is not only evaluating the content of your response, but also your modes of communicating; the organization, clarity, and conciseness of your thoughts; the appropriateness of your verbal and nonverbal communication; and your ability to pick up on visual and verbal cues.

INTERVIEW STYLES

To be prepared with effective answers it is essential that you understand the nuts and bolts of the interview core. There are actually different interview styles, designed to assess different things. By far the most common style is the *behavioral* interview, which is what we are focusing on in this book. Other styles include:

1. The *case study* interview, which is based almost exclusively on a candidate's assessment of hypothetical situations in a particular industry or field. This is most commonly used by consulting companies.

2. The *technical* interview, used to evaluate a candidate's given industry or specialized skills. If you're interviewing for a technical role, you will always be asked some of these types of questions. Often this kind of interview is done over the phone as part of a screening process before you get to the first live interview.

3. The *stress* interview, designed to gauge a candidate's response to extreme stress. Although this style of interview is rarely used anymore, you may still encounter aggressive interviewers or antagonistic questions if you are pursuing a job in the financial industry or a position that involves a security function.

THE BEHAVIORAL INTERVIEW

The premise of the behavioral interview is that past behavior is the best indicator of future achievement and success. However, we all grow, change, and learn from our experiences. When there are discrepancies between your past experiences and the job you are currently pursuing, feel comfortable highlighting those differences. Sometimes the changes you have experienced may have been welcomed, and sometimes they may not have been, but the fact that they happened is less important to an interviewer than *how you have responded to and handled them.*

OPEN-ENDED AND CLOSE-ENDED QUESTIONS

There are two basic categories of questions: open-ended and close-ended. The majority of questions are open-ended, meaning that they require full, multiple-word responses rather than just "yes" or "no" answers. For example, "Why did you join the student government/PTA/fill-in-the-blank industry group?" is an open-ended question.

There are three types of open-ended questions, which we will take a careful look at later in this chapter. Some of them are narrower and some of them are broader, but all elicit substantial and detailed information and encourage discussion. Open-ended questions also show how well the candidate understands what is being asked, organizes his or her thoughts, and verbally and nonverbally communicates a response. These questions give the interviewer context and form a basis for continued inquiries.

Close-ended questions elicit one- or two-word replies, usually "yes" or "no." While they do not reveal as much as open-ended questions, they can be highly effective and appropriate when used for verification and clarification. You can also answer these questions with more than a "yes" or "no" response when appropriate. For instance, if the interviewer asks, "If this position were offered to you, would you accept it?" you can respond honestly that it would depend on certain factors if that is indeed the case, and then share those factors. Even with close-ended questions, the interviewer is looking to assess your thought and decision-making processes. Don't feel as if you need to give a one-word answer if your true response is actually more nuanced.

STRUCTURED RESPONSES

By understanding the basic types of questions and the kinds of information that an interviewer is pursuing with them, you will be able to anticipate the general direction of the questions and think through your responses in advance of the interview. Having a framework to follow when responding to questions enables clear and concise responses, which also allows you to manage your nerves. Structured responses facilitate full, rich answers and lay the groundwork for deeper, spontaneous conversations. They will also help you keep your responses on track.

There are two methods for structured responses, which I think of as C-A-R (an acronym for Circumstances, Actions, Results) and the Inverted Pyramid.

C-A-R

With the C-A-R method, you organize a response in a straightforward, storytelling way to communicate key skills, experiences, and evidence of professional growth. You detail the circumstances, the actions you took, and the results achieved—C-A-R. This method is usually most effective when used for answers to behavior-based questions about your past experiences.

The C-A-R method is conversational. You want to provide your perspective and your reasoning; you want to show the way you think and share your reactions. In other words, you want to let the interviewer get to know you. Keep your responses concise, but make sure you connect any necessary dots for the interviewer to demonstrate how you developed a particular skill or why you made a certain decision.

Focus your response squarely on illustrating results. What is the impact of actions and results to the company, the team, the bottom line? You must think results; they are everything in the corporate world.

Let's take a closer look at this kind of structured response:

- **Circumstances:** You share a situation, task, or challenge that depicts the skill or experience about which the interviewer is querying you. You want to give the interviewer context for the story, but don't inundate him or her with minute details.

- **Actions:** This is the most important component of a C-A-R answer. You articulate what you specifically did in response to the situation and circumstances you've just detailed. Remember to highlight what you personally did to respond to the circumstances, not just what your team or group did to respond. Explain the reasons behind your actions as thoroughly and succinctly as possible. The interviewer is really seeking to understand your decision-making and thinking processes here.

- **Results:** This step is often forgotten in responses, but it's critical. Explain the outcomes of your actions, and whether or not you and your boss were pleased with the results. If the situation wasn't a complete success, don't shy away from this—instead use it as an opportunity to discuss what you learned from the situation and how you would now handle things differently.

ACTIVITY: A C-A-R WORKSHEET (CIRCUMSTANCES-ACTIONS-RESULTS)

Detail Strengths, Qualities, and Accomplishments

During an interview, your job is to make sure that the interviewer gets an accurate picture of you, your capabilities, and your experiences. Don't panic, just prepare. Complete this story worksheet to pinpoint the attributes you want to highlight about yourself and the stories you will use to demonstrate these attributes. Remember, one story can highlight multiple skills. Keep in mind your three words, your greatest strengths, and the success factors for the role. Come up with at least two stories to illustrate your key traits—think of the second and third stories as your contingency plan.

Story Title: Give yourself a quick reference to bring up the story in your mind.

_____

_____

Skills That This Story Demonstrates: List all the skills that the story exhibits about you. As you interview, you may use this story in multiple ways, so think through all the skills it exemplifies.

_____

_____

Story Circumstances: Detail the circumstances of the situation, including the specific tasks at hand and any barriers, conflicts, or obstacles you faced.

_____

_____

_____

_____

Story Actions: Detail the specific actions you took.

_____

_____

_____

_____

Story Results: What were the results of your actions? How did the story end? What did you learn, and what would you do differently next time?

_____

_____

_____

INVERTED PYRAMID

The inverted pyramid method of structuring responses is most useful for broad-based and hypothetical questions. It is similar to the approach newspapers take when organizing the content of an article: They start with a headline that gives the reader a sense of the conclusion that will be drawn, then follow it with details that lead to this conclusion, in order of importance. With the information organized this way, newspaper readers can stop reading at any point and will have gleaned the most important facts.

This is exactly how you want to think about organizing your inverted pyramid responses—for audience logic. Spotlight the most important details, facts, or anecdotes right at the beginning of your answer, supporting them with secondary and tertiary information as you wrap up your response. Your opening statement is the most direct, basic answer to the question. It is also a chance to reframe the question slightly to give the complete, well-rounded answer you want to give.

LEVERAGE YOUR EXPERIENCE

Depending on your background prior to this job search, you have different skills. If you're a parent, you are an expert at staying organized yet flexible, leading with firmness and patience. If you're a new grad, you're tapped into the latest technology. If you're unemployed, you are still experienced: The fact that the economy has been challenging or your company went through a merger does not minimize your time in the workforce and the knowledge that you've accumulated. Think about your skills, experiences, and values in a broad-picture way, note how they might be applied to the specific job you are applying for, and incorporate aspects of this whenever possible in your structured responses.

OPEN-ENDED QUESTION TYPES

Now that you understand the two basic methods for structured responses, let's take a closer look at the types of open-ended questions that compose the core part of the behavioral interview. There are four types of open-ended questions, and each is used to gather specific kinds of information. The interviewer will most likely combine different questions to fit the situation at hand. By being able to identify the types of questions and their purposes, you will be better equipped to effectively answer them.

BROAD-BASED QUESTIONS

Broad-based questions are used to explore your perspective, the way you think, and your evaluation of yourself. The opening questions of an interview are often examples of this type. They give you wide berth in determining the content of your response. The inverted pyramid approach works best when responding to them because it allows you to incorporate a wide range of things into your answer, and prioritize the order in which you say them.

If the question posed feels too broad, you may want to narrow its scope with your answer. Simply state what specific aspect of the question you will address and, if it feels appropriate, why you selected that aspect, and then proceed with your answer.

Example

"What do you know about our company?"

This question is huge, and you can take it in many directions. The interviewer wants to know such things as what your perceptions of the organization are, what research you did, and what your priorities are in terms of learning about a company. You may narrow the question by saying something such as, "I can share with you what I learned about your health initiatives, since that really inspired me to apply for this job." Another tack may be to answer by reframing the query as a similar but slightly different question. For example, you might say, "I think one of the best ways to learn about a company is to research its competitors, which I spent time doing. What I learned about one of your largest competitors in contrast to this firm is…"

Example

"How would people you worked with describe you?"

The interviewer is seeking your perceptions of how your colleagues or peers view you, listening for how you describe yourself and what this may reveal about your work behaviors and skills. You could narrow this question by, for instance, talking about a classmate's or teacher's opinion of you after presenting your semester project, or your parent group's views of you after organizing a benefit for the school, or you could answer the question from the perspectives of old bosses or subordinates, explaining the opinions of those you managed or those who managed you.

COMPETENCY-BASED QUESTIONS

Competency-based questions explore past behaviors and experiences as they relate to the job's requirements. They can also be important for the interviewer when trying to establish fit, as they can reveal some of your preferences and work habits. When answering competency-based questions, look for opportunities to connect your past experiences with your current situation to highlight why you are right for this job right now.

Competency-based questions tend to start with the phrase, "Tell me about a time when…" or "Give me an example of…" or "Describe a situation in which you…" Because these questions lend themselves to a story-based response, the C-A-R structure is very effective for answering them. Depending on the query, your answer might highlight multiple competencies. Keep your three words in mind and weave them in whenever appropriate.

Example

"Give me an example of a time when you had to deal with a difficult person and how you handled it."

This question addresses not only your interpersonal skills but also your ability to communicate, how you handle stress and conflict, and what your approach to teams is. Be aware that a question might be exploring more than one criteria or competency. When you get to the results portion of your C-A-R response, you can highlight what you learned from the situation you've been describing and the multiple skills it helped you develop.

Example

"Tell me about one of the most difficult decisions you've had to make on the job."

The interviewer is listening for the processes you used and the skills you demonstrated in dealing with a difficult situation. Follow the C-A-R model to communicate the impact of your decisions in the situation—first detail the thought process behind your actions, then describe the results, highlighting, when relevant, anything that you would do differently now having learned from the experience.

HYPOTHETICAL QUESTIONS

Hypothetical questions are based on anticipated or known job-related scenarios, tasks, or problems and can sometimes be presented as case studies. They enable the interviewer to evaluate your thought process, reasoning, values, attitudes, creativity, work style, and problem-solving approach. These questions elicit how you think, not necessarily what you know or have experienced.

When answering hypothetical questions, it is important to remember that there is not necessarily a right or wrong response, so don't give an answer just because you think the interviewer wants to hear it—such a response could indicate that you are not thinking through the nuances of the situation.

You should also feel free to give an "it depends" answer if there are other factors you would want to consider before making a decision about the hypothetical situation, and describe those factors. This kind of response can demonstrate that you don't rush to judgment and are aware of multiple possibilities in a situation.

Hypothetical questions that are presented as case studies are often more involved. They are typically real scenarios that the business has faced, though they may be new to you. Therefore, you can and should ask questions to get further information before providing your thoughts.

Example

"What would you do if a mistake were discovered during a client presentation, and you had made the mistake?"

Respond to a question such as this with an answer that reflects your maturity and sensitivity to different situations. Part of what the interviewer is assessing is how quickly you think on your feet. You might explain that in this situation you would have to consider the environment and the people in the room, taking your cue from your boss, before deciding how to respond. You want the interviewer to understand that you can read a situation and consider its nuances when evaluating how to handle it.

Example

"The company is considering a new product line in South America. Do you think it is a good idea?"

Such a case study question might take between 5 to 15 minutes to fully answer. Ask questions if necessary to gather more information about the product line, competitors, and political and geographical issues. Most importantly, weave into your answer any knowledge you already have of the region, the market, the type of product, and the company's competitors. Your response can also incorporate your assumed assessment of the situation. In such an instance, state your assumptions—how you approach an unknown situation is a core part of what the interviewer is evaluating.

PROBING QUESTIONS

Probing questions delve more deeply into a topic so that the interviewer can gather more information. An interviewer may want to investigate your rationale for the actions you've detailed in one of your responses, or seek clarity by asking you to expand on a prior experience. Probing questions widen the interviewer's context and knowledge base, and they provide information that might not be apparent on your résumé or from your previous answers.

Because probing questions do dig more deeply than other questions, they can sometimes feel uncomfortable or make the candidate nervous. This does allow the interviewer to assess your behavior under pressure, but you shouldn't assume the worst if an interviewer continues asking questions on a particular topic. On the contrary, it may be that the interviewer is genuinely interested and engaged in your responses. And sometimes probing questions aren't used to elicit information per se but to test things such as patience and poise.

Probing questions are also used to verify information. Perhaps there is an aspect to the job that is critical and the interviewer wants to make sure he or she has fully delved into this topic with you. He or she may ask about the topic multiple times and ask various follow-up questions to verify the consistency of your responses. In interviewing circles, this method is called the Rule of Threes, which we'll look at more closely in Chapter 7.

Example

After asking about a past experience, the interviewer may follow up with, "Was the client happy with the results?" or "What would you have done differently?"

When formulating your response, understand that the interviewer wants to learn about your reasoning, actions, and approach on a deeper level. It is difficult to know in advance what probing questions you may be asked, but you shouldn't overanalyze them. At this point in the interview, you will have entered into a conversation. Follow the conversation and answer authentically, again incorporating your three key words whenever possible to highlight the core traits you want the interviewer to identify with you.

Example

After asking about how your peers would describe you, the interviewer may follow up with, "Do you agree with them?" or "What do you think is your greatest strength?"

This is a way of ensuring that your key characteristics are not only the ones others see in you but also the ones you see in yourself. If there are differences in the opinions between you and your peers, explain why you may not have had the opportunity to display certain skills in that situation, or what you have done to develop those skills in other ways.

PREPARING AND PRACTICING YOUR STRUCTURED RESPONSES

You need to do as much advance work as possible to be fully prepared to answer the core interview questions. Having some basic structured responses mapped out before the day of the interview will enable you to handle the meeting with professionalism and thoroughness. It will also help you avoid tangents during the interview. It can be easy to ramble or get lost in an answer, and even worse, it can be tempting to avoid topics or experiences that feel uncomfortable. If you've prepared in advance, you'll be better equipped to confront uncomfortable topics head-on, which is exactly the sort of determination and honesty a potential employer is hoping to see.

The single most important part of preparing structured responses is understanding the success factors for the role. Take the list you've already compiled of the values and skills that the job would require for optimal productivity. If you haven't done this yet, refer to Chapter 1 for guidance on it. Once you've made the list, compile another list, this time marking down any personal and professional experiences of your own that would exemplify the success factors on the first list. Doing this will help you determine what the interviewer will want to assess, and help you plan in advance how to best spotlight your relevant qualifications and competencies. If there is a trait that is particularly critical to the job, come up with several stories that demonstrate how you possess this trait.

During the interview, you want to illustrate skill sets or professional attributes with specific stories or experiences whenever possible. Stories build connections, and they exemplify how you have handled situations. Answering interview questions is like writing a paper for a high school or college composition class: You present an answer or thesis, and then you back it up with examples. Invoke the C-A-R and inverted pyramid methods!

A word of caution: Don't over-practice or script your responses. You want to have your relevant stories and experiences top of mind, but you also want the interview to be a genuine conversation. And be prepared with stories and experiences that also highlight your personality, energy, even sense of humor. All these factors will help the interviewer assess your fit with the company.

HELP THE INTERVIEWER AND TELL APPROPRIATE STORIES

Common questions are common because often an interviewer is given a list of questions to ask and might not always think to adjust them for a particular candidate. This is when it is appropriate to give the interviewer a little help by tweaking the question slightly with your response or suggesting a similar question.

Also, boilerplate interview questions often involve queries about your most extreme experiences—the greatest, the worst, the most challenging thing you've ever faced. That doesn't mean you need to lay bare your most extreme experience if it is something difficult, traumatic, or shocking—for instance, if you were the victim of a crime or a witness to an accident. You don't want to put yourself through that in the interview, as it may rattle you, and you don't want to overwhelm, scare, or bring the interviewer to tears. Instead, choose a story that represents a trying experience and highlights the skills you demonstrated during it.

In short, you should feel confident about helping the interviewer ask you the best questions for you if necessary. Be careful not to take over the interview, but simply introducing things that feel more on topic and gently guiding the conversation is completely appropriate. Here are some sample phrases that may help you in these situations—be prepared by familiarizing yourself with them:

- I was recently asked about something very similar; I can share that story with you, which I think will give you insight into…

- I think one of my experiences would highlight ____ skill, which I know is relevant for the role. Can I share that story with you? / Are you interested in hearing about it? / Do we have time for me to tell you about it?

- Perhaps not my greatest challenge, but one that I think applies to the challenges of this job and my ability to handle it is…

- Although not the most significant, the most relevant example that comes to mind is…

ACTIVITY: PRACTICE YOUR STRUCTURED STORIES

Familiarize yourself with this list of common interview questions, and make notes on how you would respond to them with either C-A-R or inverted pyramid structured responses, then practice those responses out loud. Even better, have a family member or friend pose the questions to you if possible, probing for further information and giving you feedback on your responses. Some of these questions apply to higher-level positions—zero in on the ones appropriate for the job you are pursuing.

COMMON QUESTIONS BY CATEGORY

Overview/Personality/Fit

- How have you changed personally in the past five years?

- What work experiences have been most valuable to you, and why?

- What do you like to do in your spare time?

- What has been your greatest challenge?

- What is your most significant accomplishment to date?

- If we had to choose between you and another candidate, what is it about you that should make us choose you for the position?

- To what do you owe your success?

- Why should we be interested in you?

Tips: These types of questions give you a unique chance to highlight exactly what you want the interviewer to know about you, how you would make a great fit for the company and the position, and what sets you apart from the other candidates. Don't let this opportunity slip by: Show your value! Don't give irrelevant details; instead, relate everything you say to skill building and the requirements of the job you are applying for. Keep your answers professional and job-related.

Decision Making/Problem Solving

- If you could change a decision you have made, what would it be and why?

- What is the most difficult decision you have had to make?

- How have your education and work experience prepared you for this position?

- What types of situations put you under pressure, and how do you cope with that pressure?

- Give me an example of a problem you solved and the process you used.

- Describe a project or situation that best demonstrates your analytical abilities.

Tips: Lessons learned help us grow personally and professionally, and pressure is a part of life—the interviewer is trying to figure out what type of person you are and how you hold up under pressure. Explain how you think through decisions and develop and execute plans of action while also maintaining a big-picture perspective. Don't be indecisive or downplay tough decisions you have made. Spotlight a decision you've made that you have definitive perspective on, not one that you may feel unsure about. The interview is not the time to express uncertainty about your actions or plans for the future.

Leadership

- Name four traits that you think would be important for an effective leader. Why did you choose these traits?

- Describe a leadership role you have had, and tell me why you committed your time to it.

- Describe the ideal manager.

- What have the experiences on your résumé taught you about managing people?

Tips: We are all leaders, no matter what our role or position. A possible pitfall here is to provide examples without showing how they relate to the position for which you're applying. You can talk about coaching a kid's soccer team, starting or leading a student activity group, or organizing a neighborhood association if you show how you learned management and team-building skills from the experience. Simply make sure your examples highlight skills and characteristics required in the role.

Teamwork/Communication/Interpersonal Skills

- When tackling a project, do you like to work in a group or individually?

- Give me some examples of your qualities as a team player.

- Describe a time when you had to work with someone who was difficult. How did you handle the situation?

- What have the experiences on your résumé taught you about working with people?

- What, in your opinion, are the key ingredients to guiding and maintaining successful business relationships?

- Give me an example of a time when you were able to successfully communicate with another person, even when that individual may not have personally liked you (or vice versa).

- What is the toughest group you have had to get to cooperate, and how did you do it?

Tips: These types of questions are getting at how you interact with people and often require you to use examples where things didn't go well. Be truthful, but avoid unnecessary details. Don't retell a conversation verbatim or reveal specific harsh words or profanity you may have used. Instead, focus on explaining how the situation was resolved, what you learned, and what you would do differently now if anything. Keep things positive and don't trash anyone else, especially a previous employer or superior.

Adaptability/Initiative

- Tell me about a situation in which you had to adjust to changes that you had no control over. How did you handle it?

- What has been the most difficult part of transitioning from school to work (or work to parenthood, or from work to unemployment)?

- Describe a project or idea that was implemented primarily because of your efforts.

- Tell me about the best idea you came up with during your college, work, or caregiving.

Tips: Thinking on your feet and generating solutions are skills that are prized by any employer. When sharing these stories, avoid any personal or emotional difficulties you may have had—everything should be in reference to your career development. Absolutely talk about your accomplishments; it is fine to give credit to the team if you have established your contributions first. That way the interviewer can see both the value you bring to a situation and how you view the contributions of others. In many of these questions, employers are also looking at how you will interact with others.

Motivation/Priorities

- What are your three main priorities in life?

- What motivates you? What turns you off?

- What will you do if you are not the person chosen for this position?

- What would be the ideal job for you?

- What did you enjoy most about your past work experiences?

- Where do you think your interest in this career comes from?

- Where do you see yourself in three years?

- What goals have you set for yourself? How do you plan to achieve them?

Tips: The key to these questions is to make sure your vision for the future and professional motivation match the job you are applying for. If your ideal role is working autonomously and you're interviewing for a job that will put you on a large team, realize that expressing your desire to work independently will raise a red flag that you will not be happy in the role. Be careful about mentioning things you enjoyed about a former role that you won't have the opportunity for in this one. The employer may worry that you feel the role is below you or that you would be bored. Also make sure you answer any questions about motivation from a professional, not a personal, standpoint. Connect your answers to the position and industry at hand, and show how you will grow in the role. A hidden pitfall is saying, "I'll do any job." You may be trying to project openness and flexibility with this answer, but the employer will read it as lacking direction and uncertainty. Show not only that you can do the job, but also that it is the job you want to do. For parents, you can qualify your answer and talk about your professional priorities—that way you are not worried about ranking your family against your professional goals.

Interest in the Role/Knowledge of the Company and Industry

- What challenges are you looking for in a position?

- What type of work environment most appeals to you?

- What other types of jobs are you considering?

- What do you know about our company?

- What can you contribute to this company?

- Why are you interested in our company?

- How do you see the future of our industry?

- Who do you see as our company's major competitors?

Tips: Here is a chance to let your genuine interest shine—be prepared with your response. Do your homework, and know about any recent news or projects discussed in the media that relate to the company. At the minimum, visit the company's website before your interview and get a grasp on basic information about the company as well as the industry. As you do preparatory research, seek to understand the culture, successes, and struggles of the company and how you can fit in and contribute.

Additional Questions for a New Graduate

- Why did you choose your major?

- How did you go about choosing your school?

- How was the transition from high school to college?

- What was the best part of college?

- Tell me about an influential professor and why you found him or her inspiring.

- How would your teachers describe you?

Tips: Employers don't expect a new grad to have a lot of work experience or skills, though you may have acquired some via extracurricular activities, volunteer work, or internships. Be sure to mention specific examples. You can also use this line of questioning as an opportunity to demonstrate that you're eager, a fast learner, and that you're prepared to enter the workforce.

Additional Questions for the Unemployed

- Under what circumstances did you leave your last job?

- How have you been spending your time since you've been out of work?

- Tell me about this gap in your work history.

- Why do you think you were fired/laid off from that job?

- If you could change one thing about your last job, what would it be?

Tips: You may be dreading this line of questioning, which is why it's most important that you stay calm and confident when answering. If you weren't technically fired—you were asked to resign or you were laid off—then answer as such and explain the company's circumstances. If you were fired, be humble and focus on demonstrating how you've grown and matured since then. Acknowledge your part in it, and at the same time try to offer a reference from one of your coworkers. Never malign a former boss or employer. Instead, focus on what you learned and how you grew from the experience.

Additional Questions for Returning Parents

- Why did you take time away from the workplace?

- How will you feel about returning to the workplace and leaving your children in the care of others?

- What will be most difficult about returning to a full-time position for you?

- Are you concerned about your skills being outdated?

- Have you made arrangements for the care of your children?

Tips: When asked about your decision to stay home as a caregiver, the answer may seem obvious to you, but it is critical that you respond with confidence, positivity, and not even a hint of sarcasm. Emphasize the benefits of your decision and then steer the conversation back to the job. Do not apologize or make excuses about why you didn't return to work earlier. If you get a question about caregiving arrangements, you could refuse to answer (such questions are, after all, illegal), but it might serve you better to give a quick answer and redirect the conversation instead. You could say something like: "I've already found a great childcare provider, and I trust her completely. Now, let me tell you a bit more about..."

REFRESH YOUR MEMORY

- In the core of the interview, the interviewer will be assessing three things: Can you do this job? Do you want to do this job? Would you be a good fit for the company?

- Be authentic. If you are not yourself, then neither you nor the interviewer will be able to determine if the position is truly right for you.

- With every answer you give, the interviewer is not only evaluating the content of your response, but also your modes of communicating; the organization, clarity, and conciseness of your thoughts; the appropriateness of your verbal and nonverbal communication; and your ability to pick up on visual and verbal cues.

- Although there are different interview types, the behavioral interview is by far the most common and is the one we are focusing on in this book. The premise of the behavioral interview is that past behavior is the best indicator of future achievement and success.

- There are two basic categories of questions: open-ended and close-ended. The majority of questions are open-ended, requiring full, multiple-word responses. Close-ended questions elicit simple one- or two-word replies, usually "yes" or "no."

- Understanding the basic types of questions gives you the chance to think through and structure some responses in advance of the interview. There are two methods for structured responses: C-A-R (an acronym for Circumstances, Actions, Results) and the Inverted Pyramid.

- With the C-A-R method, you organize a response in a straightforward, storytelling way, detailing the circumstances of a situation, the actions you took, and the results you achieved. These responses are most useful for behavior-based questions.

- With the inverted pyramid method, you spotlight the most important details, facts, or anecdotes right at the beginning of your response, supporting them with secondary and tertiary information. The responses are most useful for broad-based and hypothetical questions.

- Do as much advance work as possible to be fully prepared to answer the core interview questions. Familiarize yourself with the list of common interview questions in this chapter, make notes on how you would respond to them, and practice your responses out loud.

CHAPTER 7:
SAIL THROUGH THE TRICKY PARTS

THE HURDLES, THE TECHNIQUES, THE INTERVIEWER BIASES, AND THE "SHOULD I?" QUESTIONS

You are now deep into the interview, and the questions are getting tougher. Remember, one of the things that the interviewer is evaluating is how well you respond to unexpected challenges and tough queries. Do not let a curveball strike you out! There are gracious ways to handle difficult topics and unpleasant surprises, and doing so intelligently may actually be one of the things that winds up getting you the job. Let's look at some of the nerve-racking situations that can pop up during an interview, and what you can do to diffuse them and even work them to your advantage.

THE HURDLES

An interview is a test, plain and simple, and as in any test, there are potential challenges and pitfalls. Some of these you may anticipate going into the interview, and others may be surprises that the interviewer throws at you to see how you will react. You can prepare in advance for this, though, and the better prepared you are the more effectively you'll handle any expected or unexpected difficulties.

RÉSUMÉ RED FLAGS

Résumé red flags are items that, in an interviewer's mind, highlight a potential concern in a candidate's work history. These might be gaps in employment, frequent moves, or a succession of seemingly unrelated positions. Another red flag can be having zero workforce experience, common to new grads; on the other hand, being overqualified can also count against you.

It can be uncomfortable addressing work-history gaps, especially for parents returning to work after years of raising children, or for the unemployed who were laid off or fired. But there are ways to explain these situations that put a positive spin on them and demonstrate how you grew professionally from the experiences. If you think that you are going to face this challenge in the interview, come prepared to address it head-on and with confidence.

For instance, if you were laid off, you can talk about it in a forthright manner with language such as, "The company suffered during the economic downturn, and after several rounds of layoffs, it was finally my time." If you were fired, you can phrase that experience with something such as, "My employer and I both recognized that it wasn't a good fit," and then explain why.

If your résumé reflects job hopping or unusual patterns such as too many lateral moves or even a move backward, be prepared to explain these things in an honest way that resonates with your overall job history. You might share that a job you accepted did not turn out to be the job you ended up doing, which could explain why you chose to change jobs or pursue a lateral move. Remember, you are managing your story, and you have the opportunity to put résumé quirks and gaps in a larger, more meaningful context for the interviewer.

For those returning to work after a gap caring for children or relatives, never apologize for your choices. It is a very common choice and does not mean you are less qualified than the next candidate. Focus on the skills you acquired or sharpened while working inside the home and in unpaid capacities that are valuable in the workplace. Explain how you kept up to date on the changes in your field or even with technology to show that you are ready to jump right in.

For new grads, a résumé red flag might be lack of experience. But understand that, as a new grad, you're most likely seeking an entry-level position, and employers won't expect you to have had a wealth of on-the-job experience. Instead, demonstrate why you feel that you are a good fit for that particular company's culture and mission, and point out things from your past—course work in school, internships, or club memberships—that support these assertions.

If you've been in the workforce for a while, you may encounter a different red flag: appearing overqualified for the job. This can be handled by reframing that perception and saying, "I think of myself not as overqualified, but as fully qualified." It is important to highlight specifically what makes this job appealing to you—the quality of life it would allow for, the opportunity it would give you to branch out into a new industry, whatever your reasons may be.

Keep in mind why employers are apprehensive about hiring you if you appear to be overqualified—they think it will be difficult to retain you. So consider how you can alleviate such concerns. Try, "Are you asking me this question about being overqualified because you are concerned that I may not be a long-term hire? Perhaps I can allay your hesitation by signing a contract for a term of employment, with no obligation from the company."

Another strategy is to respond to any concerns that you may be overqualified by asking the interviewer to describe the ideal candidate. Once he or she has done so, you can explain how you have the qualities they seek and give relevant examples to back this up. State that you will be able to show results in a shorter time frame due to your experience.

If possible, explain your résumé gaps, inexperience, or other red flags with stories that illustrate what you learned going through those experiences, and how they have strengthened the skills and knowledge you can bring to your next job. You want to address the inconsistencies in your past, but ultimately leave the interviewer with a clear impression of your value as an employee in the present and future. The past is the past—don't run for cover from it, but don't get hung up on it, either.

RESPONDING TO DIFFICULT QUESTIONS

It is important to remember that in addition to being a test, an interview is an evaluation and an assessment. The interviewer may ask you some tough questions to get as complete a sense as possible of your suitability for the role. Interviewers may ask about your successes in past experiences, but they are also likely to ask about your failures—this can give them valuable insights into how you confront and deal with difficult situations.

We may not be inclined to frame past experiences as failures, but be prepared to discuss some of the challenges you've faced, how you've handled them, and what you've learned from them. Certainly a merger or a round of layoffs will have been challenging. Parents and new grads will also be familiar with stressful situations such as health emergencies, sleep deprivation, tight deadlines, and high-stakes exams. Don't be afraid to translate school or family-specific challenges to skills you bring to the workforce. Be ready with at least two examples of situations that may not have gone as planned or had trying circumstances, but in which you prevailed or learned something meaningful. When citing examples from your personal life, though, seek to balance those with examples from job-related situations such as internships or volunteer work. Even babysitting jobs can be great examples of how you dealt with difficult and stressful situations with creativity, communication, and composure.

"What is your greatest weakness?" is another favorite tough question of interviewers, and it can be panic inducing—you're at an interview, and you're supposed to be demonstrating how great you are, right? So how can you be expected to jeopardize yourself by talking about your weaknesses? But the point is that if an interviewer is asking you this, he or she is trying to assess your self-awareness, honesty, and, quite possibly, poise. Don't try to squirm your way out of this question by casting a strength as a weakness—it is the standard attempt and the interviewer will usually see right through it.

I once tried this tactic by responding that my greatest weakness was that I found it challenging to delegate—implying, of course, that I was such a stellar worker I could do it better and faster than anyone else. The interviewer looked at me, shook his head, and said: "Everyone gives me that answer. Give me another." I was interviewing for my second job after college and was not at all prepared for this response. When I couldn't come up with another weakness immediately, he gave me temporary reprieve and said, "Before the end of this interview, you will tell me another weakness."

The interview continued, but in the back of my mind I was furiously scrambling. For his last question, and with a smirk on his face, he came back to the weakness query. I told him exactly what came to mind as an honest answer. I said, "If you ask my mom, she'll tell you that I often talk before I think." I then went on to acknowledge that it was true and that I recognized the impact it could have, and then I detailed specifically what I was trying to do to correct this bad habit. It prompted a genuine dialogue between the two of us, and I wound up landing the job. An employer would much rather hire someone who recognizes his or her own faults and is working to address them than someone who is oblivious to them.

Depending on the position you are applying for, the interviewer may ratchet up the intensity of questioning during the core of the interview. If the position requires a higher than normal degree of pressure or sensitivity, it may be in the interviewer's interest to get some sense of how you respond to these situations. If an interviewer gets tough, keep your cool and remember that he or she is testing your responses, not questioning you as a person. Remain personable and stay aware of your facial expressions and body language. Don't take the situation personally.

There are certain questions that may throw you during an interview, and for good reason: They probably shouldn't have been asked in the first place. But pointing that out won't win you points, so the best thing to do is what I call **Extract and Redirect**—you do not answer the question posed, but rather address it and then discuss a related topic that will still spotlight the strengths the original question was exploring. You extract yourself from the question and redirect it with a parallel response. Extracting may also involve commenting on something about or related to the question or suggesting a question that you could answer instead. This approach will help you field inappropriate or emotionally charged questions.

Below are a few such questions and some suggestions about how to manage them. These are not intended to be scripts but merely to give you ideas. Take the concepts and adapt them to your personal circumstances to make the responses yours. If you know you can handle any question thrown at you, you are more likely to manage the emotions these questions evoke.

"Do you have a special someone?" or *"What does your spouse do?"* Believe it or not, this question is far more common than it should be in interviews. Keep in mind that people may simply be curious about you and not realize that they are getting too personal or that they are asking a question that is technically illegal. There is also the possibility that they are asking it just to see how you will react. The key here is to show understanding rather than offense. That said, you do not need to answer directly. You might assume innocence by replying with, "Why do you ask?" That gives the interviewer a chance to backpedal or change the subject. Another effective response may be, "I have never been asked that in an interview before. If you don't mind, I prefer to tell you about…" That allows you to drive the content and redirect the conversation to highlight something you feel relevant for the role. Or you might use humor: "If I answer that, we may be here all night!" or "What doesn't my spouse do?" Of course, if you respond with the latter you've given away half the answer by acknowledging the existence of a spouse. Another approach is to return with questions like, "Are coworkers encouraged to socialize and get to know each other's loved ones outside of work? Are there company events that include families and spouses? I think that makes for a great work environment, and I look forward to that."

"Are you planning to have (more) kids?" Employers aren't supposed to ask whether you have kids, let alone whether you're planning to have some (or more if it's obvious that you are already a parent). One strategy here is to address the concern behind the question. "If you're concerned about my availability or loyalty, I can assure you that…" Another redirection

may be to ask, "Do many people who work here have families? Have you seen or heard of instances where that has affected their work? How did the company handle it?" This line of questioning can get current or future parents information about the company's attitude about children without revealing anything about their own situation. Be careful not to take a defensive tone as this could backfire if received as an attack.

"Do you think that it's wrong for children to be raised by nannies?" This may be a question that you have strong opinions about, but an interview is not the time to share them. Honestly, the interviewer should not be asking you this in the first place, but he or she may be trying to see how you handle a charged question. This question can be a pitfall for anyone, but returning parents and new grads face it most often. For returning parents, there is nothing wrong with sharing that you are proud of your choices and accomplishments. Another way to field a charged question is to say something such as, "I am grateful that I was able to make the choice that I did. And now I'm ready to put my skills and energy back into the workforce." Then drive the conversation back to something relevant to the job at hand, perhaps with a comment like, "Caregiving is high-stakes work, which makes me more than ready to take on the challenges I will face in the corporate world. I am very much looking forward to that."

For new grads, this question is a backhanded way for the interviewer to learn about your family plans and suss out your suitability as a long-term hire. This is one question you absolutely should not answer. A possible way to extract yourself is with: "Having a family is challenging no matter how you do it. Everybody has to find what works for him or her." You may then follow up with a redirecting question of your own, such as, "How does a team here handle it when there are differences of opinion about how to deal with things?" Or you could answer with something more closely related to the topic, such as: "How does the company handle it when employees need to care for sick parents or go on new-parent leave?" Perhaps the best move in the situation would be to clearly and simply extract yourself by saying, "That is certainly an interesting debate, but I prefer not to make judgments about other people's choices."

"What has been the most difficult thing about this transition?" This seems like an innocuous question, and it could be directed sincerely toward new graduates, returning parents, the recently laid off, or career changers. But it may be harder to answer than you think, and more of a pitfall. After all, this isn't a therapist's office. You may reframe the question slightly with something such as, "Perhaps not the most difficult, but certainly one challenging thing has been…" If you feel it is more relevant, you may also want to answer with, "Something that I expect to be challenging is…" Then you can even follow that with, "Do you have any suggestions about how to handle that in this organization?" Gently redirecting the question in these ways shows that you are thinking about your transition into this new environment and you are open to ideas about making it a smooth one.

WHEN YOU DON'T KNOW THE ANSWER

It happens that sometimes, no matter how much you have prepared for an interview, you're going to get completely stumped by a question. This might be because you simply don't know the answer, or it might be because for whatever reason you're having difficulty recalling or formulating an answer in that moment. Regardless, don't let this derail a positive discussion.

You are not expected to be robotically perfect in an interview—no one is that perfect, nor should they be. That is not what a potential employer is looking for. The most desirable candidates are the ones who are personable and relatable, and can respond to unexpected situations with confidence, intelligence, poise, and skill.

If you *should* know the answer to a question but for some reason don't, use the moment to demonstrate your knowledge about the topic in some related way. For example, if the interviewer asks you about a specific competitor's product and you're not familiar with it, state that you don't know enough about that particular product but do have opinions about this other, similar product, and then explain your opinions. You could even use the moment to comment on the industry as a whole.

If you don't know the answer to a question and can't even steer the conversation in a relatable direction, be honest about this and put a positive spin on it by taking the opportunity to ask the interviewer's opinion and advice about the topic. You could say something such as, "I hadn't thought about that before, but I'd love to learn more about it." Or, "How do you suggest I research that now that you have piqued my curiosity?" This shows initiative and curiosity and creates an excellent opportunity for following up after the interview, which we'll look at more closely in Chapter 10.

You can also gracefully reframe the situation by responding with something such as, "You know, nothing is coming to mind for me right now, but there is another story that I would like to share," and use the chance to cover something—an experience, a skill set—that hasn't yet been touched upon during the interview. This is an example of how preparing structured responses will be of tremendous help to you. If you have a number of stories and experiences at the ready, you can use them to transition between difficult moments and spotlight the primary things you want to convey to the interviewer.

Humor can also diffuse the awkwardness of not knowing the answer to a question. This isn't the time or place for thigh-slapping jokes, but if you get stuck during an interview you can laugh about it with something such as, "My goodness, that one is stumping me!" or "You know, I can't believe I can't think of this right now, but it will come to me—can we get back to this?" I took this tack when that interviewer asked me for a second weakness I had. At that moment I had a deer-in-the-headlights look and attempted a joke to distract him. I said, with humorous dismay, "Another weakness?! You mean I'm not perfect?" Even though he pressed me on the question, he laughed at my joke. This tactic doesn't always work to get out of a question, but it can increase rapport and exhibit flexibility, honesty, and relatability.

THE TECHNIQUES

There are some standard techniques that interviewers use as they're trying to get to know you. These techniques help them draw a picture of the real you—your personality, your honesty, your self-awareness, your qualifications. Let's take a closer look at three of the most common interview techniques.

THE SEVEN-SECOND RULE

An interviewer will often let there be moments of silence during an interview because it can reveal how a candidate handles a slightly uncomfortable situation, and how proactive or passive a candidate will be when confronted with a moment of uncertainty. This technique is called the Seven-Second Rule, though the silence is often for less time— even three seconds of silence can be long enough to provoke a response to it.

During an uncomfortable silence in an interview, don't begin babbling nervously about something off topic, but instead take the initiative to ask a question about what the interviewer wants of you next. "Would you like me to elaborate?" or "Does that answer your question?" might both be appropriate to ask during an awkward silence. If those queries feel too forceful, soften your tone with, "I am happy to elaborate on that if you'd like." If you have another story or experience to illustrate the topic at hand, you could say, "Would you like another example of that?" These are all entirely acceptable questions and in fact demonstrate that you are aware of the dynamics of the interview and feel at ease communicating and seeking clarity.

THE RULE OF THREES

We touched on the Rule of Threes in Chapter 6. The concept is that in order to get at the truth, an interviewer will ask several different questions around the same topic. This will help assess a candidate's true motives and values.

I was once facilitating a senior hire at a bank, and the executive responsible for the interviewing was concerned that one of the top candidates would be unhappy in the role since there was no media aspect to it. When she asked the candidate during his first interview if he minded that this role would not involve the same media exposure he'd had in his last job, he assured her that it wouldn't be a problem for him. Still concerned, on the second interview she asked him how he preferred to allocate his time on his last job, and what his favorite aspect of that job had been. Both of his responses included mentions of his interactions with the media.

The interviewer had invoked the Rule of Threes to reveal inconsistencies and known or unknown falsehoods in the candidate. He wasn't offered the job, and it was the correct decision for both of them since he truly would have missed that media aspect of his work.

Sometimes candidates don't even realize the truth of their situations, and when asked effective questions, the truth comes out.

The secret to avoiding getting tripped up by this technique is to be your true, authentic self throughout the course of the interview. If you give in to your mind games and try to be someone other than who you are, you are doing a huge disservice to both yourself and your potential employer—and you may get trapped by the Rule of Threes.

The only time you need to worry about this interview technique is when you are trying to conceal something. And if you are trying to conceal something, it's highly likely that you won't be able to avoid getting caught by the Rule of Threes. Be yourself and you'll have no reason to stay attuned to this tactic.

SEEKING INFORMATION THAT IS LESS THAN POSITIVE

One technique that is almost always used by interviewers is seeking less-than-positive information. This is how they attempt to not fall into the halo effect biases we discussed in Chapter 4. If an interviewer is getting only positive information about you, he or she may look for experiences or traits or opinions about you that aren't so positive. We have already addressed how to handle many of these tough questions earlier in this chapter.

We have all faced situations where things didn't turn out as we had hoped. If I were interviewing you, and you hadn't described or addressed any difficult situations that you'd confronted, I would be concerned. For me, that would indicate that you might not have enough experience yet for this job, or that you hadn't taken enough initiative in previous positions, or that you were risk averse, or—most importantly—that you simply wouldn't be able to handle the role. Remember, handling this part of the interview successfully is not about showing that you're perfect; it's about showing how you've dealt with difficult situations. Always conclude your responses to these types of questions by mentioning the growth you gained from the experience.

THE INTERVIEWER BIASES

There are certain interviewer biases that, while far from ideal, are fairly common. If you know about them in advance, you can leverage them to your advantage or, when appropriate, avoid them entirely. One such bias is toward physical appearance. A potential employer wants to feel comfortable with the idea of you representing the company to clients and the outside world. It's simply a fact that employers respond positively to employees and potential employees who look pulled-together—ladies, this means wearing makeup, stockings, and heels; guys, this means being sure your shirt and pants are pressed and your shoes polished, and that you always wear a tie. For more on how to dress for an interview, see Chapter 2.

Another bias or mistake interviewers often make is called the "similar to me" bias. It is the law of similarity[2] in action: People like people like them. As a result, interviewers tend to have a positive bias toward those with whom they have associations, similarities, connections, and things in common. Be sure to smile during the interview and project your genuine warmth and personality. As we discussed in Chapter 4, the rapport-building phase is an important time to establish these commonalities. If you know who your interviewer will be in advance, spend five minutes checking out his or her LinkedIn profile or other social media accounts. See what common interests you have or what people you may be connected through, and bring these things up during the interview. This small effort will encourage that positive bias toward you.

Other examples of a negative bias that you might encounter are related to age—both too young and too old—as well as against parents, especially mothers. Age comments may be addressed with references to experience, passion, eagerness to learn, and your commitment to work. You can

2 *The 11 Laws of Likability*, Michelle Tillis Lederman, 2011. Pages 130–144.

avert parenting biases with a preemptive comment such as, "I love my children and I love my work, and my former employers as well as those I volunteered with will tell you that I go above and beyond and deliver on what I promise. Having a family hasn't changed that." If a specific comment is made against children, address it, but don't become defensive. Remember that everyone has the right to an opinion. An interviewer may not even really feel negatively biased; he or she may just be trying to determine how you react to people who do.

Although it is important to depersonalize an interview experience and not interpret tough questions as a personal affront, there are occasions when the interviewer may be overstepping his or her bounds or exhibiting unfair and even illegal biases. Don't jump to conclusions, but if you are consistently feeling as if the interviewer is displaying unfair treatment or prejudices, trust your gut. It is illegal for an interviewer to ask you questions on certain topics. In the next chapter, we will look at this in closer detail.

If you are asked any of these questions, or get the sense that an interviewer is displaying an inappropriate bias, investigate his or her motives before taking further action. You don't want to come off as defensive, so approach the situation from a curious, open, and accessible perspective. In a softened and neutral tone say, "Could you share with me how this relates to someone's ability to do the job so that I can answer your concern more effectively?" If you have a medical condition that you have voluntarily mentioned during the interview, and you sense that the interviewer may have a bias in response to this, you might ask, "Do you have any concerns about what someone with this condition would struggle with on the job? I would be happy to address my abilities to perform in this role."

THE "SHOULD I?" QUESTIONS

Clients and friends often ask me what I call the "Should I?" questions, those quandaries about how to respond to certain situations that have or may come up during the interview. Should I talk about my kids? Should I talk about belonging to a fraternity? Should I talk about being laid off? Should I mention that I am engaged? It is possible to be prepared for much of what you will experience in the interview, but there are often unique circumstances that bubble up, and you may find yourself wondering how best to handle them. Usually my answer to "Should I?" questions is simple: It depends. It depends on whom you're interviewing with, what is important to you, what the job is, what the cultures of the firm and industry are.

The truth is, there are no hard and fast rules for getting an interview right, but familiarizing yourself with potential quandaries will make you more comfortable managing them when they occur. If you find yourself in doubt and cannot determine how to act, always err on the side of caution—but don't rigidly hem yourself in or suppress yourself because you think you need to, either. As we've already learned, trying to be someone other than who you are is one of the worst interview mistakes you can make.

"Should I?" questions can come up at every stage of the interview. To give you a sense of how to navigate some of the sticky situations that may arise, here's an examination of some of the ones that are most common.

TO TELL OR NOT TO TELL?

There may be some moments during an interview when you're wondering how appropriate it is to share certain information in your responses. It's my opinion that, within your comfort level, it is always best to be honest. As we've discussed in several sections of this book, if you are not fully yourself in an interview, it will be virtually impossible for you and the interviewer to truly assess your fit with the company.

When deciding what to reveal or not reveal during an interview, it is critical that you understand your rights. There are many legally protected topics that a potential employer may not ask you about, including those related to age, religion, sexual orientation, ethnic background, marital status, and family status. However, interviewers can ask questions about anything that is directly related to your ability to perform the job. If you are asked something that you feel may be unrelated to the position or is outright illegal, ask the interviewer how the information is related to the position. When you do, use a curious rather than an accusatory tone of voice.

The table below looks at some of the legally protected topics that can come up in an interview and versions of the illegal and legal questions that can occur around those topics.

LEGALLY DEFENSIBLE QUESTIONS

TOPIC	ILLEGAL	LEGAL
NAME	• What is your maiden name?	• Have you worked for this company under another name?
ORGANIZATIONS	• What clubs and organizations do you belong to?	• What professional associations related to the job are you affiliated with?
FAMILY STATUS	• Do you have any travel restrictions due to childcare? • Do you intend to have children?	• Are you able to travel domestically as needed?
MARITAL STATUS	• Where does your spouse work? • Do you wish to be addressed as Miss, Ms., or Mrs.?	• NONE

DISABILITIES	• Do you have any disabilities? • Have you ever been treated for substance addiction?	• Can you perform the job requirements with or without accommodation? • Do you have any medical conditions that impact your ability to do the job?
LANGUAGE	• What is your native language?	• What is the degree of fluency with which you speak/write any language?
COUNTRY OF ORIGIN	• Where were you born? • Of what country are you a citizen? • What kind of name is_____?	• Do you have a legal right to work in the U.S.?
MILITARY EXPERIENCE	• Have you served in the armed forces of any country? • What kind of discharge did you receive?	• What is your experience in the U.S. military? • How does your experience in the military relate to this job?
ADDRESS	• How long have you lived at this address?	• What is your current address?
EDUCATION	• When did you attend high school?	• What degree(s) do you hold? • What was your major/course of study in college? • What research work did you do in your master's program?

DISCUSSING PHYSICAL AND INVISIBLE INJURIES

A potential employer is not allowed to ask you if you suffer from an injury. If you voluntarily bring it up during the interview, then the topic is open for discussion, but it is your right to either introduce the topic or not. If you have any medical issues you want to reveal, you can do that, but I suggest only sharing information relevant to your ability to do the job. If you will need an accommodation in order to function best, then yes, you should address this in the interview. Being candid about your needs and asking the correct questions will ensure that you receive the accommodations that are going to help you be the most productive, which is in the best interest of you as well as your future employer. It may be as simple as stating that you prefer to be seated near a window because you get seasonal affective disorder, or to work in a quiet environment because you have some hearing loss. These are not unrealistic, expensive, or challenging requests to honor. And the right employer will be happy to assist you.

If you do suffer from an injury or condition that requires accommodation, spend some time before the interview thinking about how you might broach the topic with the interviewer. The more comfortable and articulate you are about your condition, the more you open the door for an honest and helpful dialogue about how the company can accommodate you.

DEFLECTING AWKWARD MOMENTS

There will invariably be an awkward moment or two in any interview. After all, it's an instance of two strangers gathering for a prearranged meeting to assess each other as deeply as possible in an extremely short amount of time. So how do you deflect and diffuse the awkwardness? If you have a good rapport established and something funny comes to mind during an awkward pause, it could be totally appropriate to share it. Humor is one of the best ways to create commonality and convey a relaxed demeanor. But if the tenor of the interview is formal, or the interviewer seems particularly reserved, refrain from using humor to dispel discomfort. And don't try to crack jokes, period, if humor does not come naturally to you. There is nothing that makes an awkward moment even more awkward than someone who is trying too hard to be funny and failing miserably.

Small talk can also help ease awkwardness, but again: It depends. If there are opportunities for natural small talk then by all means, tap them. But do not start babbling away about unrelated, minor things to fill silence or cover an awkward moment—it highlights your nervousness and calls into question how you may act in other professional settings.

You could also take advantage of a quiet moment by jotting down some notes. Remember that a few seconds of quiet does not have to translate into awkwardness. If the interviewer seems comfortable with the interview's pace and flow, then take your cue from him or her and don't try to fix a problem that doesn't exist.

You've prepared for the interview and done your homework—rely on what you know about the company's culture to determine what to do when awkwardness strikes.

It can be difficult to navigate the tough or tricky parts of an interview, but remember that the best interviews are in-depth conversations about what a job entails—the good parts as well as the bad parts—and how well you might be suited for the role. If you remain honest and authentic, you will have no problems handling these challenges, even when you find yourself wading into murky territory. Now let's move on to the next stage of the interview: your chance to ask the interviewer questions. Although this stage is often brief during interviews, it is powerful and gives you the chance to communicate your qualifications in a number of ways. We'll explore this in-depth in Chapter 8.

REFRESH YOUR MEMORY

- One of the things that an interviewer is evaluating is how well you respond to unexpected challenges. Handling difficult topics with grace and intelligence may be one of the factors that lands you the job.

- Prepare yourself in advance to field potential hurdles such as résumé red flags, tough questions, and times when you just don't know the answer.

- When questions can ignite emotions, consider the **Extract and Redirect** technique to manage those occurrences.

- Familiarize yourself with the common techniques interviewers use to get a complete picture of you: the Seven-Second Rule, the Rule of Threes, and the tendency to seek out less-than-positive information. Understanding these methods will help you prepare to respond to them.

- At times, interviewers have biases—don't let this derail you. Review some of the most frequent biases, listed in this chapter. If you know about these biases in advance of your interview, you can leverage them to your advantage and even, in some cases, avoid them entirely.

- At times, there will be quandaries or unexpected situations that bubble up in an interview, and you may find yourself wondering, "How should I respond?" The answer is: "It depends."

- You may find yourself wondering how appropriate it is to share certain information. Within your comfort level, be honest. But it is also critical that you understand your rights regarding what can and can't be legally asked of you during an interview. For a closer look at this, refer to Table 8.1.

- To deflect or diffuse awkward moments, use humor if it feels natural, or engage in small talk if the moment presents itself. You can also take advantage of a silence by jotting down some notes.

- If you have medical issues, it is fine to reveal them, but only insomuch as they pertain to your ability to do the job. If you will need an accommodation to function best, then yes, you should address this in the interview.

STAGE IV
THE CANDIDATE Q&A

CHAPTER 8:
QUERY THE INTERVIEWER
WHAT TO ASK, WHAT NOT TO ASK, AND WHY

Just as the interviewer is assessing your qualifications and compatibility for the position, you should also be evaluating whether or not the role is the right fit for you. A successful interview is a dialogue. After the core part of the interview, there will be time for you to pose any queries you may have. Ask open-ended questions that will prompt multiword answers to maximize the information you glean.

Asking questions may require a change in your thinking. A colleague recently told me that when he went on his first corporate interview after spending 12 years in higher education and then six years as a stay-at-home dad, he didn't ask a single question. Even after the interviewer encouraged him to ask questions, his response was: "No, I'm good. I have all the information I need." His thinking was that not having any questions showed that he was prepared, had done his research, and was fully able to make a decision. That was not the thinking of the interviewer, however, and he did not get called back for a second interview. Upon reflection, this colleague realized what an opportunity he had missed by not asking questions during the interview, and he never repeated that mistake again.

During the Q&A stage of the interview, you are demonstrating several things: that you have done your homework, have listened effectively during the interview, are genuinely curious about and interested in the company and the position, and understand what is important for your own decision-making process. Remember what I've been saying all along—the first interview is about getting the job, and the second interview is about deciding if you want it. During the second interview, you might focus most of your questions on determining whether or not the job is right for you. However, in the first interview, which we will look at here, you want to assess not just fit with the company but also your understanding of the job. The key to maximizing the Q&A portion of the interview is to only ask questions that you really want to know the answers to. Don't waste the interviewer's time; *use* it. You will be judged on your questions.

WHY ASK?

After responding to the interviewer's questions, you may feel as if you've said all you need to say. You may also be eager enough to get hired that you feel as if you don't have any questions because nothing would really be a deal breaker for you. But asking questions is a critical part of the interview. It puts you in an active role and gives you the chance to learn more about the position and the company, which will ultimately help you decide if you even want the job. It is often easier to ask certain questions during the interview than once you are on the job and are busy getting acclimated. Think about what is important for you to know, and make sure you ask it—this may be the only real chance you get to do so.

Asking questions also shows initiative and curiosity and illustrates your poise, confidence, and the depth of your knowledge. It further informs the interviewer about who you are, how you approach things, and what is important to you. It's an opportunity to reveal even more about your strengths and qualifications, and it shouldn't be passed up. It's also a way to deepen the rapport and sense of positive connection you have with the interviewer.

If you feel there are things that haven't been covered yet in the interview and should be, asking questions can be a way for you to steer the conversation in that direction. For instance, "Do you have any concerns about my ability?" opens the door for the interviewer to pinpoint any outstanding questions he or she may have, and gives you the chance to address these concerns with additional stories from your past experiences. If you leverage your questions well, you'll learn quite clearly what the company is looking for and what the position entails.

HOW TO ASK?

Foster a conversational tone by posing questions in a friendly way. You want to express your genuine curiosity, but you don't want the interviewer to feel as if he or she is getting the third degree. Consider the interviewer's body language and take some cues from this. Is the interviewer relaxed and open to further dialogue, or does he or she appear rushed and looking to wrap things up? Tailor your questions and approach accordingly.

If it does seem as if the interviewer wants to wrap things up, balance your desire to ask questions with your instinct to not overstay your welcome. You might say to the interviewer, "I could probably ask you several more questions, but I know our time is limited. Would it be OK if I followed up with you about any additional questions?" This demonstrates a respect for the interviewer's time and creates the opportunity for a follow-up conversation.

Be prepared with a set of questions before the interview, and consider the order in which you want to ask them—the most important questions should be asked first. The best questions are often generated by the interview conversation itself. If a query pops into your mind as you're going through the preceding stages of the interview, don't be afraid to interject it right then. If it seems slightly off topic for that particular moment, jot it down so that you can ask it during the Q&A phase. The more precise your questions are, the more they will demonstrate your interest, knowledge, and ability to be direct.

Whenever possible, ask "how" or "what" questions instead of "why" questions. "How" and "what" questions clear the way for dialogues about process and inquiry. "Why" questions can come off as demanding and will sometimes put people on the defensive.

WHAT TO ASK?

The types of questions that are appropriate for you to ask will be determined by the position you're applying for, the industry in which you're applying, the person with whom you're interviewing, the stage of interviewing you've reached, and the remaining information you're trying to gather. There are certain questions that are appropriate for second and third interviews but not for the initial discussion, and there are some questions that you should flat out avoid.

If you are interviewing with the person to whom you would directly report, you may not want to start asking about the personalities of the group right off the bat, but if you're sitting down with someone in HR, this could be an entirely appropriate question. Conversely, if it feels like a natural part of the conversation that has been unfolding throughout the course of the interview, you might ask your potential new boss about the strongest aspects of the organization or department and what things they would like to see change. These are issues that HR might know nothing about.

In general, you should stay away from discussing all employee benefits during your first interview. Immediately asking about vacation days and perks will send the message that you're more interested in those things than in the actual job. It is fine to ask what a typical workday looks like, but during your first interview don't ask how many hours a day you will have to work.

I also like to have some "back pocket" questions that are suitable to ask anyone. My favorites are those that get the interviewer talking. People respond warmly when other people find them interesting. Asking these kinds of questions can also give you real insights into how the interviewer thinks and how he or she views the job and the organization. Here are a few examples:

- What is the best thing about working here?

- What is one thing you wish you could change about your job?

- What is the best/worst part of your day?

- Why did you choose to work here?

- What do you view as the company's strengths and weaknesses compared with its competition?

All of these questions would yield valuable information about an organization's culture and would demonstrate that you too are trying to assess fit. Plus, when you get the interviewer talking and show that you are truly interested in what he or she has to say, you will increase their positive feelings toward you, too.

You may also want to ask questions that are industry or company specific. These queries will show that you have done some research and will give you more concrete information about the actual job for which you are applying. For instance:

- What are the challenges I would face in this role over the next several months?

- What are the three things you expect to get accomplished soon after completing this hire?

- Can you tell me about how the job had been performed previously and what changes you would like to see?

- Are there other job responsibilities I should know about not mentioned in the posting?

- How would you describe your ideal employee?

- I have read and heard the company culture described as _____. Do you agree, and what other words would you add?

- I read an article about increased regulation in the industry—how do you think that will impact this business?

This last question is an example of how you may incorporate your reading up on the company and the industry into a question. These kinds of questions also demonstrate initiative and a desire to understand all aspects of the company and the open position as fully as possible.

If you're interviewing with someone from HR, you may want to ask about the management style of the person to whom you'd be reporting or the general work dynamics of the group you'd be a part of. They may also be able to share about the organizational culture and if work-life balance is valued. To get a sense of the health of the organization, you can ask if recent layoffs have occurred. These are things that HR should have a good grasp on, and they can help immensely when you are determining if the job is right for you.

DON'T EVEN GO THERE!

Now that we've covered the basic guidelines of what questions to ask and how to ask them during the Q&A portion of the interview, let's take a quick look at what *not* to ask. Most things that would fall into this category are obvious, but a few of them bear repeating.

- Don't make the interviewer feel dumb. The point is not to dazzle the interviewer with your extreme intelligence, but rather to draw him or her deeper into the dialogue that you are now directing. If you do ask a question that the interviewer doesn't know the answer to, help them save face. You can lightly shrug it off with, "I knew that question was obscure, but thought I would ask." Or help them pass the buck by following the question that stumped them with, "Do you know how I might find out?" or "I am going to see if I can find out; I'll email you if I come up with anything." This would also create an opportunity for following up.

- Don't ask questions for which you should already know the answers. You should have already digested all the standard information on the company's website and in its promotional materials. Don't waste the interviewer's time—and make yourself look stupid or, even worse, lazy—by querying the interviewer on these topics.

- As I've mentioned in previous chapters, during a first interview do not ask about salary, benefits, or vacation days. Discuss these only if the interviewer brings them up. Otherwise you'll come off as calculating and interested more in the perks than the position itself.

At a certain point, you may find yourself feeling compelled to come up with more and more questions if the interviewer isn't naturally bringing things to a close. In the next chapter, we will look at how to help the interviewer end the interview and how to effectively follow up afterward.

REFRESH YOUR MEMORY

- A successful interview is a dialogue. Just as the interviewer is assessing your qualifications and suitability for the position, so too should you be evaluating whether or not this job is the right fit for you. Your chance to ask questions of the interviewer—and choosing the right questions to ask—is a key part of this process.

- During the Q&A stage of the interview, you are demonstrating several things: that you have done your homework, have listened effectively during the interview, are genuinely curious about and interested in the company and the position, and understand what is important for your own decision-making process.

- The opportunity to ask questions should not be passed up! Asking questions shows initiative and curiosity; illustrates your poise, confidence, and the depth of your knowledge; further informs the interviewer about who you are and how you approach things; and can deepen the rapport and sense of connection you've established with the interviewer.

- Be prepared with a set of questions in advance, but stay open to relevant ones that pop up during the interview. Ask "how" or "what" questions whenever possible to encourage dialogue.

- The types of questions that are appropriate for you to ask during the interview will be determined by the position you're applying for, the industry in which you're applying, the person with whom you're interviewing, and the stage of interviewing you've reached. Ask questions that will give you more information about the company's culture and the requirements of the job. Do not ask questions that will make the interviewer feel dumb, and don't waste time asking questions to which you should already know the answers.

- Unless the interviewer brings it up, under no circumstances should you ask questions about salary, benefits, or vacation days during a first interview.

- Pay attention to the interviewer's body language—if it seems as if he or she is ready to wrap things up, ask if you can follow up with further queries.

STAGE V
THE CLOSING AND FOLLOW-UP

CHAPTER 9:
SEAL THE DEAL
ENDING THE INTERVIEW AND FOLLOWING UP

The closing moments of an interview are incredibly valuable and more than simply a polite good-bye. This is your last chance to address anything that you feel has not been touched upon enough, gain clarity on next steps and how to follow up, and leave a distinct and positive final impression on the interviewer.

CLOSE WITH IMPACT

At some point while you are asking questions during your Q&A, you will wonder when you should stop asking them. You may have nothing left to ask, or perhaps you can see that the allotted time is nearly up. The interviewer may also be giving you some nonverbal indicators that he or she is ready to wrap it up. Be alert to the subtle cues—glancing at the time, organizing notes into a neat pile, pushing away from the desk, shifting to get up—that signal that the interviewer is ready to end the meeting. If things are wrapping up but you still have questions, decide which *one* question is the most vital, and acknowledge that the interview is drawing to a close by saying something such as, "I have one last question." This phrase also works when you want to indicate that you don't have any more questions.

The beginning and the end of an interview are in some ways the most important parts. The beginning sets the tone and creates an impression that the interviewer often seeks to confirm throughout the rest of the conversation. The end is the last thing that the interviewer will remember about your encounter. What is it that you want to leave the interviewer thinking?

In my experience, one of the most powerful things a candidate can do is make a closing statement. You might say, "I don't have any more questions, but I do want to make sure that I have communicated…" or simply, "I want to leave you with one final comment…" Start your statement however you feel most comfortable, and then elaborate on whatever else it is you want the interviewer to know. Be sure to incorporate your three words, and briefly touch on what you've learned during the interview, emphasizing your enthusiastic interest in the position. You can prepare your closing statement in advance, but adapt it as necessary based on the actual interview.

I clearly remember the ending of my interview for a nonexistent adjunct professor position at New York University. I was grinning with wide eyes as I emphasized that being a professor was a childhood dream that I was so excited to fulfill. I'll never forget the interviewer's flat response: "I got that." Well, it worked, because two weeks later they offered me a position that they had originally told me didn't exist.

BEFORE YOU WALK OUT THE DOOR

There are a few details you want to make sure are clear before the interview ends. Some of these things may get answered during the Q&A portion, but if not, you can ask them casually as you are getting up to leave or walking toward the elevator with the interviewer. However you fit them in, make sure to do so.

DECISION CRITERIA

Between the initial job description and what you've learned so far during the interview, you should have a pretty good idea of what the company is looking for in a candidate, but a question such as, "What do you consider the most important quality in a candidate?" will make it perfectly clear. Better yet, ask something such as, "What are the three most important attributes that you are seeking in a candidate?" This gives you the opportunity to address those specific skill sets before the interview ends. Another way to deepen your knowledge about the company's decision criteria is simply to ask, "How will you evaluate the candidates, and what will make you give an offer?" Whatever you learn from this question will be valuable information and will help you with the follow-up.

CONCERNS

As we've discussed previously, you want to address any lingering questions the interviewer may have about you before the interview ends. It is effective to just ask honestly, "Do you have any concerns about my ability to do this job?" or to say something such as, "Are there any skills that you feel are necessary for the role that I haven't highlighted for you?" Such phrasing doesn't indicate that you don't have the skills, but rather that you haven't yet explained or discussed them. This line of questioning may make you nervous—after all, why would you want to draw attention to an interviewer's doubts about you? But the fact of the matter is, the interviewer may have reservations whether or not you highlight them. If you ask about them in a straightforward way, you have the opportunity to address them and potentially eliminate them.

NEXT STEPS

Before you leave the interview, ask what the next steps are in the interviewing process. You want to find out things such as how many rounds of interviews there will be and how long the company expects to take before making its decision. This will also be an indicator for you in terms of timing your follow-up. You want to create an opportunity for that next contact with the interviewer, the company, or HR, so before the interview ends, ask whom you should follow up with. If you find out that the interviewer will be your point person for follow-up, ask if he or she prefers phone or email, and ask when you should get in touch. You may also want to ask if you can be in touch if any other questions come up for you after the interview—not only will this give you a clear frame of reference for following up, but it will also demonstrate your engagement with the process and your understanding of follow through.

SEND THAT THANK-YOU NOTE!

After the interview, following up with a thank-you note is an absolute must—send it within 24 hours. If you don't, you're signaling that you're not really interested in the job, or that you're too disorganized to focus on the correct next steps. The truth is, a thank-you note will not get you the job, but a lack of one may cost you it. The thank-you note is an easy step, and it puts you back in the mind of your potential employer.

The content does not need to be a long-winded recap of everything you discussed during the interview. Include a few key things:

- Thank the interviewer for taking the time to meet with you.

- Express your sincere, enthusiastic, and strong interest in the job.

- Summarize in one or two sentences why you are a fit for the position.

- Close with a warm but professional sign-off.

The most effective thing you can do is to personalize the letter. Referencing something you discussed or learned during the interview continues the conversation and the positive rapport that you had with the interviewer. If during the interview you created the opportunity for a specific follow-up, such as the name of a resource or a pertinent article, include that information in your thank-you note. You can pose an additional question or if one went unanswered, you could share what you found out so they have the information next time they are asked. Refresh the interviewer's memory about it, but keep this short and to the point. And whatever you do, be certain that the note contains no typos before you send it!

There has been a lot of debate about the suitability of electronic versus handwritten notes. Sending a thank-you note via email is entirely appropriate. It is fast and easy, which may make you more likely to do it. I also like the immediacy of the email thank-you note. However, if you really want a position, you might follow up a thank-you email with a snail-mail version. This will put you back in the mind of the company and hopefully keep you there. Vary the content slightly for each, and, of course, restate your interest in working for the company.

THE END OF THE INTERVIEW IS NOT THE END

You obviously won't get every job you interview for, but the process itself can be an extraordinarily valuable experience. Each time you go through the interviewing process, you will learn how to better represent yourself, articulate your strengths and assets, and demonstrate your qualifications. Don't be discouraged by an interview that does not lead directly to employment. Instead, follow up with the interviewer or HR to get feedback on how you handled the interview. In a nondefensive way say: "I really appreciated the opportunity to interview with you. In order to learn from the experience, I would value any insights you can give me about how I can improve as I continue my search." You can learn some indispensable information with such follow-ups.

Extend your interview experience by continuing to leverage it when it's through. Reach out to your interviewer with a request to connect on professional networks such as LinkedIn. If you come across something after the interview—an article, a radio segment—that directly relates to a topic the two of you discussed, extend the conversation by sending him or her a link to the item with a brief note about why you found it interesting.

Another great follow-up is to offer to help identify a candidate, as you may know others who have skill sets even better suited for the role. This may seem counterintuitive, but remember: The entire interview process is not just about getting a job, but also about potentially getting your next job. Always think about building, maintaining, and—most importantly—supporting your professional network.

Touch base regularly with the people you've met during your job search. Seek to add value to the relationship, and let them know if you're still looking for the right employment situation or where you landed. Learn and grow from all these experiences as they lead you to the job you're meant to have. The end of the interview is not necessarily the end of your relationship with the interviewer or company. You may get the job; you may not. Either way, take the opportunity to strengthen and expand your network.

REFRESH YOUR MEMORY

- The final moments of an interview are your last chances to address anything that you feel has not been touched upon enough, gain clarity on next steps and how to follow up, and leave a distinct and positive impression on the interviewer. Make the most of them!

- Close with a statement about your suitability for the role. Be sure to incorporate your three words and briefly touch on what you've learned during the interview, emphasizing your enthusiastic interest in the position.

- Before you walk out the door, make sure you fully understand what the company is looking for in a candidate, the criteria they will use to evaluate candidates, and the expected time frame of their decision. Make sure you also ask them if they have any final concerns about you that you can address, and find out the best process for following up.

- Following up with a thank-you note within 24 hours of the interview is an absolute must—if you don't, you're signaling that you're not really interested in the job or that you're too disorganized to focus on the correct next steps. A thank-you note will not get you the job, but a lack of one may cost you it.

- If an interview doesn't lead directly to employment, don't be discouraged. Follow up with the interviewer or HR to get feedback on how you handled the interview, and leverage your meeting by connecting with the interviewer on such professional networks as LinkedIn.

- Learn and grow from your interview experiences as they lead you to the right job. The interview process teaches you how to best represent yourself, articulate your strengths and assets, and demonstrate your qualifications.

BONUS MATERIALS

INTERVIEW-PREPARATION CHECKLIST

DONE	TO-DO LIST (M: MEN ONLY; W: WOMEN ONLY)
	Select your outfit and try it on with the shoes and accessories you've chosen
	Make sure your clothes are pressed
	M: Polish shoes
	W: Buy extra stockings
	W: Remove all visible piercings except single earhole M: Remove all visible piercings
	Print at least five copies of your résumé on good paper
	Pack your bag with: ■ Résumé ■ Notepad ■ Portfolio to hold résumé and notepad ■ Pens ■ Business cards ■ Info for references ■ Questions to ask interviewer ■ Breath mints ■ Dental floss ■ Small bottle of water ■ Small, stomach-friendly snack ■ W: Lipstick and extra stockings ■ W: Shoes if not wearing them there
	Go to bed early
	Set two alarm clocks
	Eat breakfast
	Leave early and check the traffic report before you go
	Check your appearance head to toe with a focus on your face; check teeth for unwanted food or lipstick
	Use the restroom before you leave home and when you arrive at the office
	DON'T wear perfume or cologne, have change or keys to jangle in your pocket, or wear anything that you fiddle with

TEN QUESTIONS YOU'D LIKE TO ASK A HEADHUNTER

Allan Goldberg has been part of the recruiting world since 1986. He has directed recruitment programs with teams of up to 40 associates, resulting in thousands of hires, and has been personally responsible for more than 1,000 hires up to the C-suite level. He has lead corporate recruiting programs in technology, sales, and research for Prudential Insurance, PepsiCo, and Gartner, and has overseen several staffing firms. He served as managing partner of Quest Resource Group, a boutique search and consultancy firm he founded in 2001. Today Goldberg is a recruitment leader with Gartner, where he oversees a team of 23. He is responsible for developing and implementing recruitment strategies for Americas sales recruiting from Canada to Brazil.

1.   **What should I know about headhunters and how can they help me?**

Working with a headhunter, also called a recruiter, will extend the reach of your job search by opening doors to opportunities you otherwise would not have known about. A recruiter will also provide you with valuable feedback on your résumé and presentation and can act as a coach and mentor during interviews, negotiations, and difficult downtimes. They can help you translate your current and prior experiences into language appropriate for their clients.

To best incorporate recruiters into your job search, it is important to know how they earn a living. The majority of search firms are either contingent, meaning they earn a commission for each job they fill, or retained, meaning they earn part of their fee up front, part during the search, and the remainder when they fill the job. In both instances, the fee is paid by the hiring company, so as a job candidate there is no need to work with a headhunter who charges the candidate a fee for their services. Since the paying client is the hiring company, recruiters will tell you that they fill jobs, not place candidates. Due to the competitive and fast-paced nature of the industry, they need to balance their time between filling or sourcing jobs and building bridges with job candidates.

2. **How do I choose which headhunters to work with?**

Not all search firms are alike. Be aware of the size and type of firm you're looking for. Is it a large national company, a small regional one, a local mom-and-pop? Does the company place people in multiple industries, or are they industry/function specialists? Do they specialize in placing recent graduates, those over 50, or are they a generalist firm? There are some companies who focus on women returning to the workforce after extended time off. Each category of firms has pros and cons. For example, large firms may provide better access to the big national and international companies, while smaller firms may have deep local connections that will work to your advantage. The important thing is to know the firm you are working with, adjust your expectations accordingly, and figure out how each firm will best fit into your job-search strategy. Keep in mind that the best headhunters will provide free advice and coaching to those candidates they want to refer to their clients, including helping to align résumés, experiences, and interview prep to meet their clients' needs.

There are so many headhunters that it can be daunting to know where to start. Here are some ideas:

a. **Look for suggestions within your existing network** of colleagues, friends, and family. Look first to people you know in your industry or profession.

b. **If you're targeting specific employers,** call their human resources department to ask if they have a preferred-vendor list of agencies with whom you can enroll. This is especially likely if you're an executive—for these positions, a job search is usually listed with only one firm on a retained, exclusive basis.

c. **If you're a recent graduate,** call the companies on your target list to ask if they work with employment agencies to hire entry-level staff, and if so, which firms they recommend. Also, ask your school's career-services office and alumni for recommendations in your target regions. Connect with the large staffing firms like Robert Half, Allegis, Manpower, and Spherion who typically have relationships with the larger employers. Look for firms like GradStaff (www.gradstaff .com) who specialize in placing college graduates in full-time, temporary, and project-based employment.

d. **If you're a returning or stay-at-home parent,** there are many new firms popping up to serve this market and provide telecommuting, project-based, or flexible work solutions for the juggling mom or dad. A few to check out are On-Ramps (www.on-ramps.com), Mom Corps (www.momcorps.com), Flex Jobs (www.flexjobs.com), Maybrooks (www.maybrooks .com), Hourly (www.hourly.com), and Work at Home (www .workathomemomrevolution.com).

e. **Search recruiter directories.** Visit your local library, where some of these resources may be available at no charge: www.rileyguide.com, www.recruiterredbook.com, www .selectrecruiters.com, www.bluesteps.com, www.searchfirm .com, www.i-recruit.com, and www.onlinerecruitersdirectory .com.

f. **Search for recruiters' profiles online,** especially on networking sites like www.linkedin.com and www.doostang

.com. To find them, do a keyword search or ask fellow members for referrals.

g. **How many agencies should I work with?** For most experienced workers, professionals, and executives, the simple answer is to work with as many agencies as your time will allow. Why? Because most employers list a job search with only one or several select agencies. Therefore, you will maximize your potential opportunities by working with more agencies. However, if you know that more than one agency is representing an employer, then work with only one to avoid misunderstandings.

h. **Are headhunters for everyone?** Remember, headhunters are paid a large fee to identify candidates with specific skills and experience. Headhunters may not be ideal for you if you are a recent college graduate or have had a long-term career break due to parenting, retirement, medical needs, or other reasons. Because your skills and experience may be too little or out of date, you may need to consider other options in these situations. Look to temporary employment agencies, which are firms that supply short-term employment opportunities that can often lead to full-time employment. They are a great way to gain entry into and knowledge of local employers, make new connections, develop and update your skills, and keep your résumé fresh during a search—not to mention that they help you boost your confidence and earn money. The five largest temporary staffing firms in the U.S. market are Adecco, Allegis, Manpower, Kelly, and Robert Half, according to Staffing Industry Analysts, Inc.

3. **What are some tips for working well with recruiters?**

    a. **Stay on their radars.** Keep in touch every couple of weeks, but value their time by using non-intrusive forms of communication such as email. And always include your résumé.

    b. **Really want to stay on the top of their list?** Offer leads about job openings or refer a colleague for a current search. What goes around comes around.

    c. **No surprises.** When you meet with a recruiter, remember that it's an interview. Show them what you'll show their client. Answer questions as best you can, and be clear, complete, professional, respectful, and truthful. Provide additional information that could be relevant, such as if you have a vacation coming up.

    d. **More is better.** Work with many recruiters, especially in a tight job market. Often recruiters will have an exclusive on a job opportunity. Connecting with several recruiters is sometimes the best way to be in the game.

    e. **Don't take it personally.** Filling positions is how recruiters make a living. Most don't have time to just chat. They'll call you when they have a good job match for you or want to give you some feedback. Remember, recruiters get paid to refer only the top two or three most qualified candidates to their clients.

4. **How have things changed?**

Today more than ever, *relevant résumés are a must.* The job-search process used to include scouring the Sunday classifieds; buying stamps, bond paper, and envelopes for your applications; and having a résumé printed at a print shop. The time and cost required meant that job applicants were selective when submitting résumés, which kept the volume of résumés received by recruiters manageable. Today, applicants can have their digital résumés sent out to tens, even hundreds of job openings at no financial cost and with minimal time investment. This may appear to increase the likelihood of connecting with a job, but the reality is that it more typically results in an increased volume of résumés received by companies, and it makes a recruiter's job more difficult. It actually decreases the likelihood of a qualified candidate's résumé being seen, especially if it is poorly written. To rise to the top of the list you need a relevant, well-written résumé that is concise and limited to one to two pages to allow for quick review. A general rule of thumb is one page per 10 years of experience.

5. **So what really happens when someone applies online, and how can I increase my chances of getting noticed?**
Applying for a job online can feel like a black hole—things go in, but nothing comes out. Résumé volume typically precludes each résumé being reviewed; there is just not enough time in the day. So most recruiters rely on "keyword relevancy" searches to identify the most qualified résumés. They will enter keywords such as "Java," "accounting," or "typing" into a database search to find résumés on which those words appear frequently. The more times a keyword appears, the more relevant it is deemed, and the higher priority it receives in the results order. It's a good tool, but it's not foolproof: Some great applicants are poor résumé writers, or simply fail to include many keywords. And under-qualified candidates can use this technology to their benefit to get their résumés to the top of the heap. So what can you do?

a. **Include keywords with frequency in your résumé and cover letter.** Instead of listing your job as "application developer," list it as "Java developer." Include keyword mentions as much as possible in the body of each job listing, as well as in your summary, core competencies list, and skill sets.

b. **Use "white type."** For example, type the word "Java" numerous times at the bottom of your résumé, highlight these words, and select white as your font color. This will essentially make the words invisible to the eye, but they remain searchable by databases.

6. **What is the value of a cover letter, and when is it needed? Can you provide some tips?**

Cover letters are a great way to provide information that is not otherwise apparent or appropriate in a résumé and can make the difference between someone selecting you or the other candidate. Use them to make it easier for the reviewer to say yes to your application. Write simply and clearly, keep the letter targeted on the job, and complement the information contained in your résumé and why the job is a fit. Use the opportunity to express your enthusiasm for the job and the company. Include a cover letter when sending your résumé directly to a hiring manager, human resources department, or someone with whom you are networking. It is less necessary when submitting your résumé to a recruiter. Here are some tips:

a. **Have someone whose writing skills you respect proofread the letter for spelling, grammar, and overall content.** If there are typos and poor grammar in the cover letter, your résumé will be pushed aside.

b. **This is the place, as opposed to the résumé, to show a little individuality.** Feel free to get a bit creative and even show a sense of humor (in good taste).

c. **A cover letter is your 15-second elevator pitch.** You need to quickly capture the attention of your audience so that they'll invite you in or at least continue on to read your résumé. Include keywords, phrases, and skills from the job description. Use **bold** and *italics* to highlight keywords or phrases so they quickly stand out.

7. **What makes a résumé effective? Can you provide some tips?**

A résumé is a key that opens the door to opportunity. It is your primary marketing tool. It should provide the right balance of quantity and quality in terms of information—just enough to intrigue your audience and leave them wanting to know more. And don't discount skills and experiences you may have gained in unconventional ways. Parents returning to work or those who have been laid off might want to include any volunteering they've done or any nonprofits they've been involved with. This is a place where new grads can highlight any clubs they belonged to, internships they completed, or athletic successes they achieved. If you're a new grad, you might include months or years for each entry on your résumé, so that potential employers can quickly see what your trajectory has been. Older workers can usually remove months—and for categories like education, perhaps even years—to keep the résumé free of unnecessary clutter and focused on skills and experiences.

a. **Focus on the high level, leaving details for the interview.** A résumé is not a job description, so make it about accomplishments and successes.

b. **Be brief and to the point.** Résumés should be as short as possible without compromising the purpose. A length of one to two pages is enough for most people. As a general rule of thumb, have one page for every 10 years of experience.

c. **Keep it current.** Focus your résumé on recent experiences—
the past 10 years. For older jobs just list company, job title,
dates, and possibly a one-line summary. Consider capturing
earlier experience, especially a previous career, as simply
"Previous experience available upon request." Remember,
complete and accurate employment details are critical when
completing a job application and at the time of interview.

d. **Be transparent.** Provide dates for all jobs, education,
et cetera. Where appropriate, include an overview of any gap
in employment due to career breaks for caregiving or other
reasons—be sure to include relevant volunteer or other work
experience during this period. If you've had an extended
period of temporary employment, list it as one entry titled
"Temporary or Consulting Employment," and then list
the firms you worked through. Lack of transparency sends
a message to recruiters that you're hiding something and
creates an opportunity for mistrust. This calls the wrong type
of attention to your experience.

e. **Don't overstate the obvious.** In your résumé objective/
summary use a phrase like "experienced professional"
instead of "over 25 years of experience." Although seemingly
counterintuitive, at the recruiter level there is a definite
bias favoring less-experienced candidates, even if it's an
unconscious one.

f. **Make it easy for the reviewers to say yes.** They should see the
relevancy of your résumé in 15 seconds or less. Remember,
your audience likely has to sift through hundreds of résumés,
so highlight areas that will help them focus on yours, such as
keywords, successes, and competencies.

g. **Make it relevant to the job description.** Scan the job description or ad for required industry experience, skills, and training/education, and any action words. Be sure your résumé includes as much of this same language as possible, including acronyms.

h. **Be consistent.** Poor spelling and grammar are résumé no-nos. A less obvious no-no is the inconsistent use of formatting. If you use a period to end a bullet point once, use it throughout. Make sure dates are aligned, and use the same formatting for headings, company names, and job titles. Using Microsoft Word tables and templates can be helpful when organizing your résumé.

i. **Keep it understated.** Don't get fancy with a résumé. Unless you're applying for a creative-type job, keep the résumé traditional.

8. **What tips do you have for telephone and video interviewing?** Phone interviews are typical today, especially as a first interview with both agency and corporate recruiters. Video interviews, while less frequent than phone interviews, are nevertheless a part of interviews at all levels in today's expense-conscious world where geography can be a barrier to the initial and subsequent interviews. In either case, it is important to remember that it's a real interview, so take it seriously. The goal is to get invited for an in-person interview. But talking on the phone isn't as easy as it seems, and video interviews can be awkward. Prepare well for both, from researching the company to grooming properly and having a résumé in front of you when you interview. Practice ahead of time if you can. Set the stage, clean away all clutter, and clear the room (and the house if possible) of kids and pets. Make sure you use a phone with good service to eliminate static and

dropped calls. Disable call-waiting to minimize interruptions. Phone calls and even video calls can feel informal, so be aware of your "ums," "uhs," and "OKs." Remember to smile and sit up straight to project a positive image and energy, to listen carefully, and to keep answers brief and on topic.

9. **How do I handle compensation with a headhunter?**

It is important to know that you and the recruiter are on the same side. It is in his or her best interest to get you the highest salary possible—both because the commission is based on it, and because he or she wants to make placements that result in long tenure and growth. Competitive compensation is critical to this goal. A headhunter will be your advocate and help handle the negotiations. A few guidelines to help that process are:

- **Be open.** It's fine to ask for details about the job before providing your salary expectations. However, headhunters will not represent a candidate who does not share salary history and expectations—they have a responsibility to provide this information to their client.

- **Be flexible.** Don't state a bottom line too early in the conversation. Say that you will consider all the factors in determining your salary flexibility (e.g., location, hours, benefits, responsibilities, et cetera). Headhunters will assess whether you are "placeable" in part on the reasonableness of your salary expectations in the current market and how flexible you are during salary discussions.

- **Be realistic.** Headhunters will be well informed about market/client salary ranges. However, they won't share this information with you. Their goal is to keep both the client and job candidate in a reasonable (closable) place. They want to manage everyone's expectations well before they get to a final offer so that they are confident the deal will close. Remember that the market supply and demand for the position determines salaries, not the job candidate.

- **Be informed.** Do not enter your job search relying solely on the headhunter to guide you. Do your own research in advance and know the salary range in your area for the job you're seeking. The Internet is a great place to start. You can find lots of market salary information on a variety of websites, including www.salaryexpert.com, www.jobstar.org, and www.salary.com. These sites typically provide general and broad data. Just as important, keep in mind that your target range should also include a consideration of the current market conditions and your marketability.

10. **What are some of your best tips?**
   a. **Thank-you notes are a must.** They can be the difference between your landing the job or someone else getting it. But keep your note brief, spell personal and company names correctly, and absolutely have two people proofread it before you send it. Sending via email is fine.

   b. **Continue to network your way in.** Even after submitting your résumé online, use your network to increase the likelihood that it will be reviewed. It can be powerful when someone hears your name from multiple sources. But be careful not to overdo it. Two mentions are great, but you shouldn't seek out more than three.

   c. **Go to the CEO's office.** Not literally of course. Send your résumé to the CEO or president. No, they likely will never see your résumé. But most companies, especially large ones, will have a follow-up process in place for résumés sent to top executives. An assistant will likely forward them to the head of human resources, who in turn will hand them to someone responsible for recruiting. Since the résumés have come down from the CEO's office, they will very likely be reviewed at this level. Why? Because no one wants to be in the position of not having followed up on a résumé from the CEO.

TOP FIVE TIPS FOR MAKING THE MOST OF CAREER FAIRS

Attending a job fair is a proactive way of getting to know companies or industries you're interested in. It's also a great way to make contacts. Here are five things you can do to make the most of the experience.

1. **Have a game plan.** You have to have a clear objective in order to accomplish it. Manage your expectations of career fairs— companies do not typically interview or hire on the spot. Consider these goals for your plan:

    a. **Meet the company.** This is part of your non-Internet research. Chat about what you learned while exploring the company beforehand online, such as new-hire programs, training opportunities, and company culture. Show up at the fair early to give yourself a chance to connect with the recruiters when they are at their highest energy levels. Staying late and offering to help carry out boxes as the fair closes will also give you a chance to chat more casually with the recruiters and to be remembered.

    b. **Obtain business cards.** Meeting a direct contact from a company will give you a name to reference in a cover letter and a number to call with questions. Every business card you're given is a possible contact and will help build your network, whatever role you end up in. Companies often send representatives from both the business side and HR to the fair, so when you meet someone make sure you ask what they do and don't assume you know. If a recruiter doesn't offer his or her card, ask for one. If the recruiter doesn't have any business cards, you can write down contact info on the back of your card, or have a notebook handy for just this purpose. Don't be afraid to ask for an email address.

c. **Hand-deliver your résumé.** Bring many copies of your résumé with you and give them out in a way that increases your chances of being contacted about the role. Before the fair, print out one or two job descriptions from the company you are targeting and review them so that you can refer to them directly when you meet that company's recruiter. If the jobs have ID numbers, know them—the recruiter will likely write those job numbers on your résumé and give it to the people responsible for filling those roles. Understand that your résumé will go into a stack of more than 100 others, so you may not be contacted. Manage your expectations, but increase your odds by delivering your résumé in a targeted fashion.

d. **Get a clearer view on a specific job.** When you have a targeted job in mind, you can seize the opportunity to learn more about that role from the recruiter. Ask if the role is a new one, and if it isn't, find out what made the last person successful in the position. See who the recruiter thinks would be an ideal candidate for the job, and share a bit about how you have some of the qualities mentioned. And show your enthusiasm! If the person at the event doesn't have much information about the job, you can ask for the name of someone who does, and create a follow-up point of contact for after the fair.

e. **Learn from your competition.** You can learn a lot by listening to those around you. What questions do they ask? How do they pitch themselves? Strike up a conversation with those you feel are impressive and learn from them. Ask how things are going for them and you may hear about other opportunities, job, or fairs that interest you. Ask for a business card, too—this is one more person to add to your network.

2. **Research the companies.** You can almost always find out what companies will be at a career fair weeks in advance. This gives you ample time to go to each company's website, review job openings, and even apply online before the fair. Also, seek to connect to a current employee before the event. You can then plan your time at the fair around the companies you are most interested in working for and possibly have a name to drop during your conversation.

   Referencing a specific job and asking related questions will maximize your face-to-face time with the recruiter. Tell the recruiter why you want to work for this firm, and you'll stand out from the crowds of people who simply print out a bunch of résumés, put on a suit, and show up at the fair. When you discuss something specific, most of the time, the recruiter will flag your résumé for follow up.

3. **Be prepared.** Being prepared for a job fair does not simply mean printing out enough résumés. In addition to researching the companies, you also want to:

   a. **Have questions ready.** Think about what questions you want to ask the recruiter to probe further about what you learned during your research online and through talking with current or past employees. This is your opportunity to interview the company and investigate the position. Be careful not to make the questions too hard or obscure—you don't want to make the recruiter feel stumped or dumb. Also, don't interrogate the recruiter by asking too many questions. Keep things conversational and be considerate of the recruiter's time and the long line of people behind you. Be remembered, but for the right things.

b. **Know your pitch.** Most conversations will start in the same ways, which means that you can be prepared for what you're going to say. Have your lines down. Your opening pitch should include the following elements:

"My name is…"

"I am a…"

"I am seeking…"

Chances are high that the recruiter will then follow up with questions about why you are qualified for the roles you are seeking. You should be ready to respond to these questions with two or three sentences. For instance, you might begin with:

"In my work as a _____, I have…"

"I believe my training and experiences would benefit [insert company name] in the following ways…"

4. **Look and sound the part.** Fit is one of the criteria for any company. There are many factors that go into assessing fit, including dress, language, and nonverbal signals.

a. **Dress for success.** Look the part. Appearance and first impressions make a difference. Wear a suit and review Chapter 2 for the specifics on workplace attire expectations.

b. **Speak the same language.** There is slang for every industry, but it usually doesn't translate far beyond that industry. New grads should leave the slang behind, but also avoid being too formal: If you are used to the sir/ma'am address, drop it. You must be mentally athletic and adapt to the situation. You can chat, but don't talk to the recruiter as if he or she were your buddy. Treat the recruiter with professional respect.

c. **Communicate strongly with your body language.** Research shows that up to 93 percent[3] of what you communicate is physical, not verbal. Don't make your potential employer uncomfortable by appearing robotic and rigid. Be mindful of all the components of your message. Present a strong but not crushing handshake. Always smile to convey that you are personable and have positive energy.

5. **Follow up.** A career fair is just the first point of contact with a company or recruiter. It should definitely not be the last. Create follow up. Write thank-you emails, contact anyone whose name has been passed along to you, and reach out to the other candidates you met as well. When contacting people you met at the fair, mention something the two of you talked about to refresh their memory about who you are. Your follow up will underscore your interest in working for the organization. Even if you already spoke to a current employee, ask your contact from the career fair to connect you with the network—the more people you're in touch with, the better your chances are for furthering your relationship with the company.

Even if you decide afterward that you are not interested in certain positions you may have discussed at the fair, maintain the contacts you made there. Take a long-term perspective during your job search. These people may not help to connect

---

3 Mehrabian, A. (1981). Silent messages: Implicit communication of emotions and attitudes. Belmont, CA: Wadsworth.

you with your next job, but they might be exactly your point of contact for the one after that.

STRATEGIES FOR OVERCOMING THE TOP FIVE RÉSUMÉ RED FLAGS

1. Being or Appearing Overqualified

Often those switching careers or looking for a job following unemployment have too much experience, education, or both for the position they are applying for. When an applicant has more years of experience than the job requires, it raises red flags for the employer such as: Are you exaggerating your experience? Will you require more pay? Will you leave quickly for a better opportunity? To manage questions about being overqualified, consider the following techniques:

- **Take salary off the table.** Make it clear that you are flexible and that what you earned in the past is not relevant to your current job search. Share with the interviewer that you have many factors that impact your interest in the position.

- **Address the potential concerns up front.** Bring up the topic first. Ask the interviewer if he or she has any concerns about you performing in the role, then highlight your accomplishments, flexibility, and ability to thrive in a team environment. State that you are looking to contribute and are pleased that you may bring more to the table than other candidates, which would allow you to hit the ground running.

- **Explain your reasons.** Tell the interviewer your reasons for being interested in the role, even though it appears that you are overqualified for it. Think this through beforehand so you'll be prepared. Is it because the job will give you a good work-life balance? Is it because you will find it fulfilling to thrive in a role for which you have all the qualifications?

- **Lighten your résumé.** Consider removing dates or positions from your résumé so you don't overwhelm the interviewer with your experience. You can share some of the relevant information during the interview after you have made a strong impression. If they ask you why you have done this, state that you didn't think those experiences were relevant to the role, and you wanted to highlight your more recent experience.

- **Be humble.** Reassure the interviewer that though you are an experienced candidate, you realize that you have to prove it to each employer. State that you look forward to the opportunity to grow in the company but are comfortable starting in this position.

2. Gaps in Employment

This is particularly challenging for stay-at-home parents. Employers are looking for confirmation that you have remained up-to-date in your profession. Be prepared to answer industry questions to highlight your current industry knowledge. Show that you are so interested in your field that you found ways to apply your skills or read up on the current industry even while you were unemployed.

3. Frequent Relocation

Perhaps your spouse is in the military or academia and you've moved around a lot. You need to be aware that an employer's worry about relocation is that it will happen again, and you will have to leave your position if hired. If you know that you will be stationed for a period of time, share that. If asked how long you plan to be in the current location, state, "The *hope* is three to five years, possibly longer." I never advise lying, but by saying "hope" you remove any falsehood from your statement. If you are asked, "Where do you see yourself in five years?" talk only about your career goals as they relate to the company and the role, not about location, family status, or unrelated education planned.

4. Job or Career Hopping

In today's times, moving around frequently is not as frowned upon as it once was. In fact, staying at one job too long may actually work against your candidacy if you have not shown growth in your role. That said, changing jobs every three years is more acceptable than every one or two. Companies are making an investment in you and want to think you will stay around.

If you have academic degrees that do not closely match your work experience, or if you have multiple degrees and vast work experience that are not consistent with one other, this could indicate to an employer that you don't know what you really want to do, and that you're not just job hopping, you're career hopping. A couple of ideas for handling these situations are:

- **Create a targeted résumé.** Select the content that best suits the position you are targeting; highlight the skills, functions, and industries that are most applicable. Remember, you do not have to include every single job on your résumé. Gaps are sometimes easier explained than hopping.

- **Tell your story and connect the dots.** Present your experience as a continuous progression during which you gained skills and experience along the way. For instance, you might explain a transition with, "I wanted to learn about customer service, so I took a job in …" Sometimes it isn't obvious why you made certain decisions—help the interviewer understand the skills you've gained in each role and how they relate to the job you are now seeking.

5. Lacking Career Direction

Because new graduates lack a track record, employers may worry that you are just testing out the waters in a certain field and are willing to take any job. Desperate job seekers are not highly desired workers. Employers are looking for motivated workers who truly want to be working for that company, in that industry, in that role. If you lack career direction, take the time to figure out what you want to do so that you can commit to the position and the industry. Ask yourself what you would do if you had $5 million in the bank. Think about the things you do for fun or because you want to, not because you have to. What do you volunteer for? Is there a career in that for you? Once you are clear on your passion, you can look at your skills and determine how they can be leveraged. You will also be more compelling in an interview if you can explain why you want to do a particular job. Let that enthusiasm and passion come through. Once you decide what you want to pursue, consider these ideas to help direct your career:

- Make a career plan for the next two to five years.

- Build industry experience by continuing to work or volunteer.

- Maintain a network of contacts. Keep in touch with the people you met at college, parent groups, or previous jobs.

- Get active and join local industry organizations such as the chamber of commerce.

- Be creative—if you can't find the job you want in the industry you desire, look elsewhere. No nursing positions available at a hospital? Try a local school, a doctor's office, a nursing home, or even a service for home health aides.

FIVE WAYS TO GET THE MOST FROM YOUR CAREER CENTER

Michael Malone has spent more than 20 years in higher education at competitive institutions including Columbia University, UC Berkeley, Northwestern University, the University of Pennsylvania, American University, and Stevens Institute of Technology. During his tenure, Michael has worked in both undergraduate and graduate career centers, having led the Career Education and Advising team at Columbia Business School for six years, and serving as the Managing Director of the Career Management Center at the Kellogg School of Management at Northwestern University. He is currently the Associate Dean for MBA Programs at Columbia Business School. Michael earned his M.S.Ed in Higher Education Administration from the University of Pennsylvania, and his B.A. from Fordham University.

In the 2014–15 academic year, almost 3 million students will graduate from U.S. colleges and universities with an associate's or bachelor's degree, and nearly 1 million students will complete a graduate degree. That's a population the size of Los Angeles (and one that has increased by more than 30 percent in the past 15 years) hoping to land career opportunities, and likely leaning on the career centers of these colleges and universities. But exactly what are these career centers able to do to help you—and, more importantly, how can you get the most from them?

1. **Set the right expectations.** Career centers are not like Walmart—you don't pick up a job off the shelf—nor are they matchmakers like e-Harmony. They are more like fitness facilities: They have equipment and offer training, but they can't lift the weights for you if you want to get stronger. Career centers are typically good at a number of things that can support how you manage your career, including providing information about market and industry hiring trends, helping you to practice skills you'll need to successfully land jobs, and fostering relationships with

organizations that might want to hire you and for whom you might want to work. Each of these areas will contribute to you developing a feasible plan for yourself. Remember that you have to be responsible for putting together *and* following through on a plan, and that the career centers can provide elements and support.

2. **Get to know yourself.** Career centers can offer assessments and analyses about what makes you tick. Why is this important? Because you have to know what you like, what you are good at, and what motivates you in order to know what you bring to the table as a job candidate. Learning more about your personality preferences, interests, motivators, skills, reaction impulses, and inspirations will better inform what industries, companies and jobs you target. Skip this step and you will spend a long time spinning your wheels, chasing after different ideas.

3. **Get to know your target.** In order to connect effectively with an employer, you need to know what's important to them, what they value, what motivates them, and what skills they need. Some students do well with self-assessment and know exactly what they are good at—this is necessary, but only half the equation. The other half is knowing about the potential employer. Researching different industries—and the companies within those industries—helps you understand what organizations fit your interests, skills, motivators, and values. Career centers are especially adroit at supporting industry research and typically curate data and analyses that you won't find elsewhere. How much is enough research? Although it differs by individual, a good benchmark is if you can clearly articulate the following: how your skills and abilities would enable you to make a contribution to a specific organization, how that specific organization differs

from its competitors, and whether the work you would be doing at that organization would give you energy.

4. **Market yourself.** Once you've found the intersection of your interests/goals/energy-giving activities and an organization's needs, it's time to tell them. Another sweet spot for career centers is helping students prepare their portfolios of marketing materials, ranging from standard items like résumés and cover letters to minutiae such as helping with introductory or networking emails, thank-you notes, and other forms of correspondence. They are also great resources for interview training. Career centers can help you make sure that your marketing materials accurately represent your previous experience and convey what is most relevant to the prospective employer. Your marketing materials should be tailored to the industry, and even to the specific organization, you are targeting. Career centers have sample résumés, cover letters, recordings of mock interviews, and more, all of which you can and should leverage.

5. **Have a consigliere.** Career centers have seen lots of students and have been through all kinds of market conditions. Although they can't predict a specific outcome for you, the collective experience of a good career center staff can help inform your strategy and tactics, provide valuable feedback about how you can improve, and help you weigh the pros and cons of a particular approach or opportunity. Like any good consigliere, career centers can help you make a highly informed decision. The work of getting into the career center, finding the right person to help you, developing and refining a plan, and executing that plan, is up to you. If you work with a career center in a proactive, positive manner, there are potentially long-term benefits. Many career centers provide some type of support for their alumni, ranging from databases of alumni contacts to workshops and seminars to proprietary job

boards and individual coaching. Establishing a good relationship with your career center can help ensure that you get a lifetime of benefit from your undergraduate or graduate institution.

FIVE TIPS FOR CHOOSING AND WORKING WITH A CAREER COACH

Lisa Chenofsky Singer helps individuals, corporations, nonprofits, and entrepreneurs become more successful by developing and refining their career strategies. Lisa is a strategic thinker with a tactical approach. She offers executive, leadership, and career coaching services, guiding clients on career decisions and enhancing their capabilities. Lisa is an Adjunct Professor and Curriculum Developer for Rutgers University, and has taught at Montclair State University and Union County College. Lisa's certifications are in Executive Coaching, Career Transition, and Leadership Development and Coaching. She is certified in Myers-Briggs Type Indicator (MBTI), FIRO-B, and Hogan Assessments. Lisa has her master's in Organizational Communications with a bachelor's of Art in Psychology. Lisa has her own executive and career coaching practice, Chenofsky Singer and Associates LLC.

When you meet someone new, it's one of the most frequent questions: "What do you do?" Your career contributes to your quality of life, but also to how you define yourself and to how others define you. What we *do* enables us to use our talents, influence others, and earn our livelihood. Careers over the past few generations, however, have evolved. It used to be that one could join an organization and remain there for 30-odd years. These days, most people will have five to eight career shifts. How do you navigate such changes with confidence, and without losing your sense of self? Understanding what you enjoy doing, developing and using your abilities, and assessing the needs within the marketplace will enable you to remain marketable—and it's where a career coach can come in handy.

A career coach is similar to a sports coach—he or she helps you improve, turning abilities into strengths and developing skills that enable you to grow. A coach can help you avoid time-consuming job-search mistakes and expedite the process. Consulting with a career coach can be extremely valuable if the coach is selected correctly, and a waste of time and money if not. Here are five tips for helping you decide if a career coach is right for you, and if so, how to choose the best one.

1. Clarify Your Big-Picture Goals

Managing your career strategically begins with a plan for the short and long terms. The first step in the process of deciding whether or not you're going to work with a coach is determining exactly what your priorities are. Where do you want your career to go, and how do you want help achieving those goals?

A career coach with extensive experience will help you set and achieve your goals, targeting opportunities that are aligned with them, and helping you strengthen your resilience and maintain motivation despite ups and downs. You will learn how to work through and overcome potential barriers while staying focused on your objectives, and you'll learn to identify and surmount self-sabotaging behaviors.

An experienced coach can help you broaden your job-search criteria based on your marketable skills and experiences. There are times when a career coach can help you identify and/or clarify your goals to fine-tune them for your desired outcome. The coach can provide valuable objectivity and customized support, but you are going to get the most out of any coaching experience if you've clearly identified your goals and motivations for seeking out a coach beforehand.

2. Drill Down and Identify What You Want on the Micro Level

A career coach works with you to identify the changes you are seeking in your professional life, and then helps you devise a strategy for realizing them. Some of the areas coaches can be adept at include, but are not limited to, the following:

- Identifying the types of positions and responsibilities you enjoy and are capable of performing

- Identifying your possible transferrable skills and targeting the best ways to articulate these

- Identifying development needs that will help you strategically prepare for future opportunities

- Aid you in creating and presenting your best presence in the marketplace through your résumé and use of social media

- Identifying your network and helping you establish and maintain a robust connection to it

- Improving your storytelling skills to benefit your networking

- Rethinking job-search strategies

- Identifying references in preparation for the job search

- Preparing for interviews and following up afterward

- Strategizing answers for the difficult interview questions, and managing anxiety around this

- Negotiating packages and compensation

- Navigating the onboarding process once you've landed a job

Again, you're going to have the most rewarding and satisfying experience with a coach if you can clarify for yourself beforehand and then articulate to him or her exactly what it is that you want help with.

3. Know What a Coach *Can't* Do

Many people believe that a career coach will land them a new job. A career coach does not place people in jobs—this is what recruiters and headhunters do. A career coach can't tell you where you should work, isn't necessarily going to leverage his or her own network to help you find work, and can't get you a job. What a coach *can* do is help you define actionable steps that will get you where you want to go, and then help you chart that course. Think of a coach as an accountability partner— you need to answer to someone in order to stay the course and achieve your stated goals. A good career coach will sustain the focus you have around your career strategy, even beyond the job search.

4. Find Your Fit

Selecting the right career coach means finding someone who will challenge you in a beneficial and productive way. Selecting the wrong one can be disastrous. Coaches who are properly trained and adhere to a professional code of ethics understand that coachees need to assess their options in order to find the appropriate coach. Not every coach is right for every coachee, and an experienced, ethical coach will often even give referrals to coaches who might be a better fit for your needs. Here are some tips for finding the person who is right for you.

a.   Generate a List of Recommended Coaches

Ask colleagues and friends if they have ever used a career coach, much in the same way you would ask your network for recommendations for service providers such as doctors or dentists. Go to the International Coach Federation website and search through the coaches listed in your area. Read testimonials from former clients and research any mutual connections you may have with any coaches to get second opinions from people you trust.

b. **Assess Experience, Background, and Style**

Inquire about, listen to, and understand a coach's philosophy, energy, style, and approach. What sort of thought leadership will he or she bring to the relationship? Do the coach's social media and website presences resonate for you? What are the coach's credentials and educational background? What certifications does he or she have? Does the coach's roster of previous clients align with where you are in your career development and how you are hoping to grow? And, just as imperative, what sort of coaching style are you looking for? Do you want someone understated and tactful, whose style is to move through a session by posing lots of questions to you? Or do you prefer someone who will take a more charged, even slightly confrontational tack, and whose style is to directly challenge you?

c. **Conduct Informational Interviews**

Schedule time to speak with prospective coaches in order to learn how they've helped previous clients—what were clients' goals, and what did they achieve through working with the coach?—and to gauge what your chemistry might be like with each individual coach. Selecting a collaborative, attuned, adaptable coach is critical toward achieving your goals—but so much of this comes down to chemistry. You need to choose someone who makes you feel both at ease and inspired. Most career coaches will engage in a preliminary call to determine if the working relationship might be a good fit. Ask yourself immediately after the conversation, "How did that feel?" If you were excited and inspired and made perhaps even a bit nervous by your discussion, chances are it will be a good match, and that the coach will engage and stretch you to grow beyond your comfort zone. Selecting a career coach who will challenge you properly is critical.

5. Keep Things on Track

Your career coach is your personal sounding board. Coaching should be a safe environment in which you share your thoughts and feelings and fine-tune your communication style to achieve your desired outcomes. Ensure that your coach is ethical—if you have questions about this, one good place to start is the International Coach Federation's website, which spells out its code of ethics.

As with any engagement, you need to understand your goals and the value the service provider is adding. If you are frustrated or confused, ask for clarification. A good coach-client relationship is interactive and responsive, and a coach will be collaborative, engaged, and adaptive.

And don't make your coach a crutch. Track your progress and be aware when you've reached your goals. Then evaluate whether or not you want or need to continue working with the coach. One of the reasons it's so important to have clearly defined goals going into a coaching relationship is because it's one of the things that will help you determine when the relationship has run its course.

What you are looking for in a job may change over time as you evolve, but what you learn during career coaching is often applicable again and again, regardless of the situation. Career coaching is, in large part, about personal development within a professional context, and more often than not the skills and experience you gain during coaching will stay with you for many years to come.

In the short term, working with a career coach often results in a higher income, a shorter job search, better decisions, and greater happiness. Even if you are adept at seeing the big picture and thinking strategically, it is often hard to turn your strategic eye inward and allocate time for self-reflection. During a work transition—when you might finally have the time and motivation for introspection—it can be natural to revert to panic mode. But when you have a game plan, you can calm down, focus, and perform.

Even if you don't work with a career coach at this time, being aware that there are professionals who have training and certification in this field may be just the safety net you need to feel comfortable and move forward with your journey.

PHONE INTERVIEWS, VIRTUAL INTERVIEWS, AND UNCONVENTIONAL APPROACHES

Although the traditional interview is still the prevailing type when it comes to job searches, there are more and more instances of new techniques and unconventional approaches. Just as the workplace is changing in the 21st century, so are the methods and tactics companies are using for finding and assessing employees. In this section, we'll take a look at phone and Skype interviews that take the place of in-person interviews, as well as several interview modes that are shattering the conventional approach all together.

PHONE CALLS AND VIDEO CHATS: MASTERING THE REMOTE INTERVIEW

These days, there is an extremely high degree of professional mobility and a widespread comfort with all the devices that let us lead on-the-go, mobile lives. As a result, more and more employers are turning to remote interviews, either over the phone or via Skype, when an in-person meeting can't be arranged. This is especially common for technical roles and situations where the team is in multiple locations; a virtual interview is also often used as a pre-interview screening, to determine if the company wants to set up an in-person meeting.

Generally speaking, there are no downsides to doing these types of remote interviews, though Skype is preferable to the phone simply because seeing someone's face has a dramatically beneficial impact on perception. If you are not familiar with Skype, don't be intimidated—it is quite simple to use and, best of all, it's free. However, if for some reason you don't have the ability to use Skype, by all means arrange to conduct the interview over the phone.

In both cases, you should dress and position yourself exactly as if you were going to an in-person interview. Women, put on lipstick, and men, trim your beard. Both genders should wear your best job-interview shoes. (Yes, wear shoes—they impact how you carry yourself even while seated.) Sit in a chair at a table, with a pad of paper and a pen, and lean forward in the chair so that your energy is in your body. This will all positively influence how you present yourself.

And remove any distractions from your environment! Decide where you'll sit in advance of the interview so that you'll be somewhere quiet, preferably even with a door closed, in order to fully focus on the conversation. Beware of external noise in your chosen space including kids, pets, nearby construction, and leaf blowers and lawn mowers.

If you are doing the interview over the phone, consider having a mirror propped in front of you so that you can see your reflection and make sure it's animated and energetic. This enthusiasm will be transmitted by your voice. Since the phone won't allow you to communicate with your body language, remember to add words and sounds to fill in the gaps. An occasional "Hmm, interesting" or "I see" can go a long way to show that you are paying attention and are focused and interested. Silences are more challenging over the phone than in person or over Skype. If during the phone interview there is a silence that feels awkward, simply ask if the interviewer needs a minute to take notes, or if he or she would like you to expand on your response. Attempt to minimize environmental noise as much as possible: Put the dog outside and send the kids on a playdate.

If you are conducting the interview via Skype, test out your camera angle before the interview begins. Be aware of what the interviewer will see behind you and remove anything that will not reflect well on you professionally. Have the interviewer's camera view on screen to remind you of what is visible to them. While the interview is taking place, make sure you look directly into the camera when you are talking, and maintain direct eye contact as best you can—it will keep you connected to the conversation and projecting confidence.

OUT-OF-THE-BOX INTERVIEWS AND UNCONVENTIONAL APPROACHES

As workplaces and working styles continue to morph, more and more companies are adopting nontraditional interviewing styles to help them assess who the best employees are for their needs.

Whole Foods has a multistage application cycle that takes about 60 days to complete. As part of that, candidates have group interviews with a panel of managers, recruiters, and employees so that the Whole Foods teams can have direct input about who comes on board to join them in the workplace. In situations like this, the criteria a company is looking for are often more about character—previous experience is less relevant. Whether or not your values and attitude are the right fit for the company are critical factors being assessed.

At the innovative employee-rewards company Next Jump, thousands of job applicants are rigorously screened for what the company calls Super Saturday—the day each year when the top candidates are flown to one of the Next Jump offices and undergo a full roster of skills exercises, informal meals with current Next Jump employees, and team challenges for which the applicants work on a problem together in small groups and then submit their solutions to a panel for review.

Other leading companies are evaluating candidates via a series of points-based tasks and even asking prospective employees to perform skits. In these situations, the same basic interview-prep tenets apply, even if the actual interview itself is dramatically different. Embrace the powerful chain reaction discussed right at the very beginning of the book, in Chapter 1: Knowledge, Clarity, Confidence. If you're prepared in this way, you'll handle the unconventional interview with aplomb.

WHOLE FOODS

www.cosmopolitan.com/career/interviews/a32661/interview-insider-whole-foods-career-jobs

NEXT JUMP

blog.nextjump.com/culture/super-saturday.html

NOTE FROM THE AUTHOR

Thank you for reading *Nail the Interview, Land the Job*. In writing this book, I sought to ensure candidates broadened their thinking around what is part of the interview process. The process starts before even getting the interview, and, truthfully, it never ends. Remember, though you may not get the job you are interviewing for, you may be thought of for the next one.

Use the book as a reference guide. As you evolve in your career, different aspects of the book may become relevant. *Nail the Interview, Land the Job* was written to help the broad spectrum of job seekers. But not all candidates have the same challenges, which is why I paid special attention to the issues facing new graduates, returning parents, and the recently (and involuntarily) unemployed.

No matter how comprehensive my attempt, there are always more questions. I love hearing from readers and welcome you to contact me to connect or ask me any unanswered questions. There are a few I am often asked, which I answered below, but please don't let that stop you from reaching out. Good luck with your search.

Thanks for reading!

Michelle

AUTHOR FAQS

Q: What is your background?

I like to tell people I am a recovering CPA—which is true. I spent the first decade of my career in various accounting and finance roles from auditor to M&A analyst to financial consultant to being the only woman on the trading floor—with a few stops in between.

I am a career changer. I majored in accounting and double minored in writing and communications. I had a vision for what I wanted my life to be, and the power suit and corner office were part of that vision. Plus, I am really good with numbers. The route seemed obvious, until I got everything I wanted (including that corner office on Wall Street) and realized I was unfulfilled.

Working in corporate, specifically finance and consulting, I had more than a few complaints over how people managed, communicated, and pitched. Wanting to explain how to be more effective in the workplace was the impetus for founding Executive Essentials, www.executiveessentials. org. I always say, "I teach how to not make all the mistakes I made and saw."

There is more to my background, and you can check me out at: www. michelletillislederman.com/meet-michelle.

Q: Have you written any other books?

Yes, I have written two other books and always have another in my head, so stay tuned.

My first book was *The 11 Laws of Likability: Relationship Networking… Because People Do Business with People They Like.* It is available currently in eight languages as well as in e-reader and audio formats. www.amazon. com/gp/product/0814416373

My second book was a gift to help veterans enter the civilian workplace and is called *Heroes Get Hired: How to Use Your Military Experience to Master the Interview.* The content is free for veterans and their spouses at www.heroesgethired.com.

Q: Are there opportunities to work with you live or one-on-one?

There are many ways I work with people including group training, speaking, and one-to-one coaching. The two most common ways for live support are 1) being hired by an individual's organization and 2) attending a live speaking or public event. However, I do keep a few slots in my calendar for private clients. See below for additional options.

For those who would like to go through their organization, you can reach out via www.executiveessentials.org or email info@executiveessentials.org.

If you would like to see where I am speaking, events are listed at www.michelletillislederman.com/meet-michelle/upcoming-event.

If you would like to attend my live two-day program, you can learn more about it at www.relationshipdrivenleader.com.

If you would like private coaching, you can see noncorporate options at www.michelletillislederman.com/speaking-coaching/coaching.

Q: Do you have other resources for the job seeker?

I am always thinking about additional ways to help and hearing what you need is a great source of ideas. Connect with me via social media (see next question) and join my email community to be notified as new resources become available. I will be creating a downloadable Interview preparation checklist soon at www.michelletillislederman.com.

You can read through my blog at www.michelletillislederman.com/blog for tons of articles. I also send out a weekly one-minute video (I call them Success Shorties) on a range of topics relevant throughout the job interview and all the way up the ladder. You can see past videos on my YouTube channel at www.youtube.com/user/MichelleLederman. I welcome your comments and feedback.

Q: How can we connect with you?

I love when people reach out, and I welcome you to do just that. When you connect, let me know why and how you found me. Personal notes to me get a personal note back. I ask for your patience in response time as the volume has increased immensely over the years. I do my best to respond to everyone. Different ways are:

Twitter: www.twitter.com/mtlederman
Facebook: www.facebook.com/MichelleTillisLederman
LinkedIn: www.linkedin.com/in/communicationexpertspeaker
Website: www.michelletillislederman.com/contact/
YouTube: https://www.youtube.com/user/MichelleLederman

Q: *Is there anything we can do to help you?*

I love when people ask that question! I encourage you to keep asking people that question and to always have an answer ready when someone asks you.

So, obviously, my answer is yes! A great way to help me is by providing a review on Amazon at:

www.amazon.com/Nail-Interview-Land-Step---Step/dp/0996507809

I also welcome you to engage with me online via Twitter, Facebook, and LinkedIn (links above) as well as my email community at www.michelletillislederman.com

INDEX